THE GLOUCESTERSHIRE REGIMENT

WAR NARRATIVES
1914 - 1915

Compiled by

Captain R. M. GRAZEBROOK, O.B.E., M C.

The Naval & Military Press Ltd

Reproduced by kind permission of the Central Library,
Royal Military Academy, Sandhurst

Published by
The Naval & Military Press Ltd
Unit 10 Ridgewood Industrial Park,
Uckfield, East Sussex,
TN22 5QE England
Tel: +44 (0) 1825 749494
Fax: +44 (0) 1825 765701
www.naval-military-press.com
www.military-genealogy.com
www.militarymaproom.com

In reprinting in facsimile from the original, any imperfections are inevitably reproduced and the quality may fall short of modern type and cartographic standards.

INTRODUCTION

THE following accounts of the 1st and 2nd Battalions of The Gloucestershire Regiment in France and Flanders were finally compiled in 1923 with the help of the surviving officers and men who had served with the Regiment at the time.

The object was to make as accurate a record as possible of the doings of the Regiment in those early days of the War, before the facts were completely forgotten.

Already, after a lapse of eight years, it was found hard to recall every detail, and especially of the exact moves of the various companies during that terrible week of continuous fighting in the Ypres Salient in 1914. A portion of the War Diary for the period was lost, and the part that does remain to us is in places painfully brief. There is practically no first-hand information that was actually written at the time, with the exception of a few of the orders and messages received in the field during the Retreat from Mons.

The record of casualties sustained by the 28th, and also by the 61st, was particularly hard to compile, because often no accurate returns were, or could be, kept during the days of incessant fighting. Officers, N.C.O.'s and men were far too tired and worn out to think of returns, even if the necessary information could have been collected. It must be remembered that in many cases, especially in the First Battle of Ypres, the Officers or N.C.O.'s whose duty it would have been to make out the casualty lists, were often missing themselves, and that their successors probably hardly knew the names of all the men in their platoons or sections. Drafts, when they arrived, would go straight up into the line, and no record might have been kept to show to which Company each man was posted.

In working out the daily casualties, every care has been taken, but it must be realised that they do not pretend to be absolutely correct. The numbers of men shown as going sick are only approximate. It has been found that the casualties as given (1) in the returns to the A.G. Branch in France at the time, (2) by the Record Office, and (3) in the official War Office list ("Soldiers died in the Great War"), all differ, and mistakes have been found in each list. It is not believed greater accuracy can now be obtained.

In order to make the varied and chequered fortunes of the two Battalions into continuous reading, it has been necessary to say something of the general situations, and to give the movements of neighbouring units. It must, however, be borne in mind that this only purposes to be a record of the Regiment for the Regiment.

The maps at the end, for reasons of economy, simply show the more important places mentioned in the narratives. To those who wish to follow in more detail the moves of the Regiment, are recommended the following official maps issued by the Ordnance Survey at Southampton: the 1/250,000 sheets of N.W. Europe (4 miles to 1 inch) for the Retreat from Mons, the 1/100,000 sheets of France and Flanders (1½ miles to 1 inch) for the more stationary operations, and the 1/40,000 sheet 28 of Belgium (¾ miles to 1 inch) for the struggle east of Ypres.

Thanks are due to the Record Office at Warwick, and to all those others who have kindly come forward with information and diaries, or who have read over and checked the narratives.

SHANGHAI,   R. M. GRAZEBROOK.
April, 1927.

1st BATTALION
THE GLOUCESTERSHIRE REGIMENT
"1914"

1st BATTALION
THE GLOUCESTERSHIRE REGIMENT
"1914"

1st Aug. AUGUST, 1914, found the 1st Battalion of the Gloucestershire Regiment under canvas at Rushmoor Bottom, Aldershot, carrying out its annual training with the remainder of the 3rd Brigade of the 1st Division.

Rumours of an impending European War on a previously unknown and gigantic scale had been day by day becoming more persistent, and it was soon realised that if Great Britain became involved, and was to dispatch an expeditionary force overseas, orders for mobilisation could scarcely be withheld much longer, and that the 1st Division, forming as it would a portion of any such force, would naturally be one of the first units to receive such orders. When, therefore, the 3rd Brigade were suddenly instructed on the afternoon of Saturday, August 1st, to strike camp and to march back to its own station at Bordon, no one was much surprised.

The next few days, before the British Government actually declared war on Germany, were spent in preparing in a quiet way for the rush of the expected mobilisation.

At 6 p.m., August 4th, much to everyone's relief, orders for a General Mobilisation were received. The following day was to be considered the "first day of mobilisation," and everything had to be completed by midnight, August 7th/8th.

The Battalion was much under strength, both in officers and men. Two captains, seven subalterns, and about 600 men were required to bring the numbers up to the then War Establishment. Reservists, however, rushed back to the Colours, and poured into the Depôt at Bristol, and on the 6th August, 580 men, under Captain J. E. Ruck, were dispatched to Bordon. Captain N. F. Baynes, Lieutenants W. V. Churchill-Longman and T. R. A. Morris, and 2/Lieutenant H. Cox, all of the 3rd (Special Reserve) Battalion, together with 2/Lieutenants W. F. Watkins, H. E. Hippesley and M. Kershaw, of the Supplementary List (Reserve of Officers), also joined the Battalion on this day. As there were no captains available in the Regiment to complete the numbers required, Captain A. St. J. Blunt, of the York and Lancaster Regiment, and Captain A. G. McC. Burn, of the East Surrey Regiment, who were on leave from their foreign service battalions, were attached to the Gloucesters for duty.

On the 7th, on the arrival of Lieutenants K. A. R. Smith and R. K. Swanick (3rd Battalion) with five reservist corporals, the Battalion was over strength, and the companies could be reorganised and the men told off into their platoons and sections. As far as possible, all reservists were posted to their old companies, so that they might serve once more alongside their old comrades. On this day, August 7th, orders were received from the War Office for each Battalion to send to their depôts one captain, two subalterns, and fifteen sergeants or corporals as personnel to commence the immediate training of a new unit—the forerunner of the New Armies. Captain W. P. Pritchett, Lieutenants Smith and Cox, five sergeants and ten corporals accordingly left for Bristol the same evening. The war strength of battalions was reduced at the same time to allow for these officers and men remaining in England.

By midnight 7th/8th August, with the exception of twenty men still required to complete the Base Details, the Battalion was fully mobilised and ready to move. The

8th Aug. amount of work carried out in the three days allotted was prodigious, and the fact of it being done so smoothly speaks very highly for the Battalion Mobilisation Scheme, made out for the most part by the Adjutant, Captain A. H. Radice. Peace equipment had all to be handed in, and war stores issued—no small matter, especially where the transport was concerned; swords and bayonets sharpened; pay-sheets, conduct sheets, and other documents prepared; medals collected and handed in; personal kits packed either to accompany the Battalion or to remain stored somewhere until the end of the War; etc., etc. The draft horses were received from the Remount Depôt on the 6th, and the riding horses on the following day. The total number of animals to be taken overseas amounted to 56. The breaking-in of these horses was no easy task, especially as a number of the transport personnel were new to the job. The harness and equipment, when issued from the Mobilisation Stores, was all in small pieces, and had to be put together, softened, and fitted to the various animals. These, having been accustomed to the more comfortable civilian harness, in many cases did not take kindly to the tight and new military impedimenta, and a certain amount of comic relief was afforded when the transport turned out for its first short route march.

A few weeks earlier, during the summer training, the 2nd Division had carried out a practice mobilisation. To bring their units up to war strength without calling up the reserves, battalions and batteries, etc., from the 1st Division had been absorbed, and it had been possible to see units complete for war and fully equipped with their transport. This test, without doubt, materially assisted the Aldershot troops and the staff, when the time came for the rapid calling up of men and animals.

On August 7th it was learnt that the first day of movement was to be Sunday, 9th. It was not, however, until the 12th that the 3rd Infantry Brigade actually left Bordon. The extra days were occupied as far as possible by carrying out field training and musketry for the benefit of the newly-arrived reservists, some of whom had not served with the Colours for many years, and to whom the short modern rifle was an unknown weapon.

Special guards had also to be furnished to protect the power stations, post office, etc., from any possible enemy interference. A further batch of reservists—30 in all—arrived on the 10th, thus completing the Base Details. This reinforcement of 100 men was put under the command of Captain A. A. McLeod, and having finished off the packing of the Battalion's stores and property at Bordon, they would be ready to follow the Regiment overseas when required.

On August 11th the Battalion was inspected by the Brigade Commander, Brigadier-General H. Landon, C.B., and during the day the following preparatory orders for entraining were issued to Companies:—

SPECIAL ORDERS FOR ENTRAINING.

The Battalion will entrain in two trains, as follows, hour of parade for each train loading will be notified later. Attention is directed to "Aldershot Command Instructions for Entraining," issued to Companies.

1st Train loading.   Train No. 406.

Headquarters (less Senior Major, Regimental-Quartermaster-Sergeant, Transport Sergeant, Pioneers, Half Stretcher Bearers, 2 S.A.A. carts, 1 watercart, 1 tool wagon, spare horses, Senior Major's batman and horse, 3 R.A.M.C. personnel, and 2 train G.S. wagons).

A and B **Companies**.

2nd Train loading.   Train No. 410.

Remainder of Headquarters.
Machine Gun Section.
C and D **Companies**.

Before leaving Barracks the following fatigues will be detailed :— **11th Aug.**

A and C Companies—
- (a) Two hold parties of 1 N.C.O. and 5 men each.
- (b) 1 Officer and 30 N.C.O.'s and men for loading transport.
- (c) 1 Officer and 10 men for loading baggage.
    - (a) will report to Embarkation Officer on arrival at docks.
        - (b) and (c) will, on arrival at Bordon Station, form up at the entrance of the station, and the officer in charge will report to R.T.O. on the platform.

After marching on to the platform, entraining will begin at once from both ends of the train, 8 men to each compartment.

Companies will take up compartments for their fatigue parties.

This order was followed by a Special Battalion Order :—

In accordance with instructions issued to Companies—

    1 a.m. to-morrow, 12th inst.   1st Train loading.
    2.40 a.m. to-morrow, 12th inst.   2nd Train loading.

All ranks will carry 3 days' rations on the person.
Ammunition will be issued before parade.
Transport will be loaded at 5 p.m. to-day.

The departure from Bordon was carried out without event in the dark and early hours of August 12th, and without the bands and flag-waving which was usually associated with the departure of troops for a theatre of war.

The two trains arrived at Southampton at 5 a.m. and 6.30 a.m. respectively, and the Battalion proceeded to embark in the SS. *Gloucester Castle*. During the embarkation one draft horse was injured in the head, and had to be left behind, otherwise there were no troubles.

The following list shows the officers who accompanied the Battalion overseas. Lieutenants Churchill-Longman and T. R. A. Morris were surplus to establishments, and remained with Captain Ruck to take charge of the boys and unfits who had to be left at Bordon

HEADQUARTERS—
    Lieut.-Col A. C. Lovett, Commanding Officer.
    Major J. O'D. Ingram, Senior Major.
    Capt. A. H. Radice, Adjutant.
    Lieut. M. W. Halford, Transport Officer.
    Lieut. D. Duncan, Machine Gun Officer.
    Lieut. W. J. Hewitt, Quartermaster.
    Capt. A. W. Howlett, R.A.M.C., Medical Officer.

A COMPANY—
    Capt. R. E. Rising, Commanding.
    Capt. A. St. J. Blunt (Y. & Lan. Regt.), 2nd in Command.
    2/Lieut. D. Baxter, No. 3 Platoon.
    2/Lieut. H. E. Hippisley (S.I.), No. 4 Platoon.
    2/Lieut. M. Kershaw (S.L.), No. 2 Platoon.

12th Aug.

B COMPANY—
    Capt. G. M. Shipway, Commanding.
    Capt. N. F. Baynes (3rd Bn.), 2nd in Command.
    2/Lieut. B. F. R. Davis, No. 7 Platoon.
    2/Lieut. A. D. Harding, No. 8 Platoon.
    2/Lieut. R. M. Grazebrook, No. 6 Platoon.

C COMPANY—
    Capt. W. A. M. Temple, Commanding.
    Lieut. H. E. de R. Wetherall, No. 9 Platoon.
    2/Lieut. Hon. N. F. Somerset, No. 10 Platoon.
    2/Lieut. W. F. Watkins (S.L.), No. 12 Platoon.

D COMPANY—
    Major R. M. S. Gardner, Commanding.
    Capt. A. G. McC. Burn (E. Surrey Regt.), 2nd in Command.
    Lieut. F. H. McL. Young, No. 13 Platoon.
    Lieut. J. A. L. Caunter, No. 16 Platoon.
    Lieut. R. K. Swanick (3rd Bn.), No. 14 Platoon.
    2/Lieut. W. S. Yalland, No. 15 Platoon.

The three other battalions in the 3rd Infantry Brigade at this time were the 1st Queens, 1st South Wales Borderers, and the 2nd Welch Regiment. Of these, the S.W.B's joined the Gloucesters in the SS. *Gloucester Castle*, the Welch embarked in the SS. *Braemar Castle*, while the Queens sailed with Brigade Headquarters, the Staff of which was composed as follows:—Brigadier-General H. Landon, C.B.; Captain J. B. Jenkinson, Rifle Brigade (Brigade Major); Captain G. N. Dyer, The Queens (Staff Captain).

The SS. *Gloucester Castle* sailed at 12.10 p.m., 12th August, and after dropping the pilot in Sandown Bay, Isle of Wight, put to sea at about 3 p.m. for a destination known only to the captain of the ship. Land was sighted at 11.30 that night, and at about 1 a.m. the following morning the troops began to disembark at the docks of Le Havre. As these were the first troops to arrive at this port, the preparations for disembarkation were somewhat scanty, and with the exception of a very few French Infantry Reservists, there was no labour available. There was a certain amount of delay, therefore, especially in unloading the transport, as all the animals had to be slung. Whilst this was being done, the Battalion assembled in a large cargo shed, and the men were able to snatch a few hours of sleep. At about 6 a.m. the Battalion fell in, and Colonel Lovett read to the troops His Majesty's message of good wishes. Lord Kitchener's letter, which is given below, was also distributed to all ranks:—

> You are ordered abroad as a soldier of the King to help our French comrades against the invasion of a common enemy. You have to perform a task which will need your courage, your energy, your patience. Remember that the honour of the British Army depends on your individual conduct. It will be your duty not only to set an example of discipline and perfect steadiness under fire, but also to maintain the most friendly relations with those whom you are helping in this struggle. The operations in which you are engaged will, for the most part, take place in a friendly country, and you can do your own country no better service than in showing yourself in France and Belgium in the true character of a British soldier.
>
> Be invariably courteous, considerate and kind. Never do anything likely to injure or destroy property, and always look upon looting as a disgraceful act. You are sure to meet with a welcome, and to be trusted; your conduct must justify that

welcome and that trust. Your duty cannot be done unless your health is sound. So keep constantly on your guard against any excesses. In 13th Aug. this new experience you may find temptations both in wine and women. You must entirely resist both temptations, and, while treating all women with perfect courtesy, you should avoid any intimacy.

     Do your duty bravely.
     Fear God.
     Honour the King.

              KITCHENER,
                Field-Marshal.

Guided by French Boy Scouts, a start was then made with cookers, watercarts, and Maltese cart for No. 1 Rest Camp, near the French forts at Ste. Adresse, some four miles from the docks, on the high ground to the north of the town. The Regiment received a tremendous reception from the townspeople, as Lord Kitchener had anticipated—all the more enthusiastic as the French nation had feared in the first days that Great Britain might not, after all, come to their aid in the time of their need. Those who formed part of the original British Expeditionary Force are not likely to forget the welcome and the kindness of their Allies in those early days of the War. Flowers, fruit, cakes, wines of the country, were pressed on all and everyone, and with results at all times amusing, and at times disastrous.

The Rest Camp, which even in later days could not be called luxurious, proved to be a large, flat stubble field, where a hundred bell tents were put at the disposal of the Battalion. Here, however, one more valuable day was spent in practising fire control and fire discipline. And there is no doubt that these final touches helped to increase the remarkable fire effect of the 1914 Army, which so astonished the Germans during those first months of the War. The rapidity and accuracy of the rifle fire brought to bear upon them caused them to believe the British Army was equipped with an unlimited supply of machine guns.

Two interpreters—Leroux and Duval—reported for duty this day. Both were private soldiers in the French 104th Regiment of Infantry, and were wearing the well-known blue and red uniform of the " poilu " of that day. These men were of the greatest help, especially when arriving, after the day's march, in a fresh village, where they would arrange for billets for the officers and men, and do what buying of provisions was possible.

By August 14th the 1st Division had completed its landing, and the 3rd Infantry Brigade had orders to proceed to the theatre of war the next day. Reveille on the 15th was at 4 a.m., after a very violent night of thunder, wind and drenching rain, and by 8 a.m. the entraining point at the docks was reached. The train allotted to the Regiment consisted of fifty 3rd class coaches and closed wagons—the latter marked " 30-40 hommes, 8 chevaux," and largely used in France for the transportation of troops. Four hours were allowed for entraining, but the whole Battalion, complete with its transport, did it well under an hour. It was not, however, until 12.39 that the train slowly drew out of the siding, and the Battalion commenced the next stage of its eventful journey— once more into the unknown. The train arrangements were said to be several years old, and so complete and carefully worked out had they been, that every man, horse and wagon reached its destination to time, and with no confusion or mishap. It is stated that to avoid altering the wonderfully prepared timetables, certain trains travelled up empty towards the point of concentration, when the units to which they had been allotted were for some reason or other not available at the time.

All along the line the Battalion received the same enthusiastic welcome, and gifts of fruit and flowers. At Rouen, which was reached at about 5 p.m., the train drew up, and the men were given an hour for refreshments and washing. One man was transferred sick to the French hospital in the town. The journey was continued *via* Amiens, St.

16th Aug. Quentin and Wassigny, and the main railhead at Le Nouvion was reached between 6 and 7 o'clock on 16th Aug. Here the Battalion cooked breakfast in a field to the west of the village, and at about 10 a.m. marched off south, through the Forest of Le Nouvion, to the 3rd Infantry Brigade concentration billets about Leschelles.

The Gloucesters' area lay round about the hamlets of Le Tilleul and Dohis, at the south-west corner of the forest. Brigade Headquarters were at Leschelles itself, about 1½ miles away, and the remainder of the Brigade were to the south-west of Le Tilleul. The Battalion was ordered to furnish two piquets, each of one platoon under an officer, to watch the approaches from the east. Instructions were also issued as to traffic within the concentration areas, and as to the movement of civilians. A curfew was imposed, and persons could only move from village to village with a permit issued by the local *maire*.

The next three days, whilst the concentration of the British Expeditionary Force was taking place, were spent mostly in route marches, in improving the defences of the billets, and in practising the manning of the alarm posts by day and night. Lectures were also given at Brigade Headquarters on the general situation as it was then known, and on the tactics it was expected would be most favourable in the coming struggle.

The outposts were reduced on the 17th to two examining posts, the remainder of the two platoons acting as inlying piquet. French troops were actually occupying an extended line of outposts further to the north, to cover the concentration. On the 19th the Battalion received its first mail from home. Orders were also received late that night for the Brigade to move on the following day to new billets.

Reveille on the 20th was at 5 a.m., and at 8.45 a.m. the Battalion commenced its march north towards the Belgian frontier. Marching at the head of the 3rd Brigade, and *via* Le Nouvion, the Regiment covered a distance of 8½ miles, arriving at its next billet at Beaurepaire soon after noon. Although this was only a short march, it must be remembered that the summer of 1914 was abnormally hot. The continual heat, dust, and long days of marching, together with all other privations of modern warfare, especially at the beginning of a campaign, were most trying, even to the serving soldier who was in the pink of condition after the summer's training at home. To many of the reservists, some of whom were naturally unused to such a life, the strain proved too great. No matter how pluckily the man stuck to it, there were times when one too old for the strain, another physically unfit, and another perhaps with bad feet or legs, had to fall out. This first march found out a few of the weak spots in the ranks, and ten men were sent sick to hospital. The billets at Beaurepaire were found to be far from good. The Companies were very scattered, and the men were very crowded in the various farm buildings. The night, however, passed quietly, and at 8.30 a.m. the next morning the march north was resumed. This day the 1st Division moved along two roads. The 2nd Infantry Brigade acted as a right flank guard, and marched on Avesnes, whilst the remainder of Division continued north through the villages of Cartignies and Dompierre to Dourlers, about 13 miles away. The Gloucesters formed part of the advanced guard which marched in the following order :—Cyclist Section, The Welch, Gloucesters, one section R.E., and one section R.A. The whole of the 3rd Brigade billeted in Dourlers—the officers mostly in the inns and houses, and the troops in the outbuildings.

By the 21st Sir John French's concentration south of Maubeuge was practically complete, and the next day the British Army was to commence to carry out the mission allotted to it by the French Commander-in-Chief, General Joffre. It is necessary at this stage to view the situation as it was then known, and to follow briefly the moves of the opposing armies which led up to the Battle of Mons. The Germans had entered Brussels on the 20th August, and were known to be advancing south-west, apparently with the idea of enveloping the left flank of the Franco-British armies and of separating them from the Belgians, who had been forced back on to Antwerp. The strength of this most westernly German army—the 1st, commanded by General von Kluck, was not as yet known, but it was believed to consists of three corps.

The plan of the French Higher Command was to meet the enemy first on **21st Aug.**
the line Charleroi-Mons, and after breaking his attack, to assume the offensive,
to swing round on the fortress of Namur to the north-east, and so to assist in the
reoccupation of Brussels, and enable the British Army to connect up with the Belgians.

The British Army at this period consisted of the I Corps (1st and 2nd Divisions) under Sir Douglas Haig, the II Corps (3rd and 5th Divisions) under General Grierson, succeeded on his untimely death by Sir Horace Smith-Dorrien, and the Cavalry Division under General Allenby. The III Corps (4th Division and the 19th Infantry Brigade) was not as yet formed. The first task assigned to the B.E.F. by Joffre was to advance north of the Sambre towards Soignies, and to protect the left of the Fifth French Army.

On the 21st and 22nd, therefore, the British Army proceeded north, and crossed the Belgian frontier to take up a line from Binche through Mons and along the line of the canal to Condé.

To return to the Gloucesters and the rest of the 3rd Brigade. No orders for the following day's operations had been received on the 20th, but during the night several contradictory instructions came through. Finally, at 3.15 a.m., August 21st, information was received that the Cavalry Division had been in touch with small bodies of hostile cavalry about Mons, and that the Division would continue its advance *via* Maubeuge.

The 3rd Brigade Group formed once more the advanced guard to the Division, and was on the road at 5 a.m. The vanguard, under Major Pilkington, XV Hussars, consisted of one squadron XV Hussars (less two troops), Cyclist Company (less one platoon), and one Company and the Machine Gun Section of the Welch Regiment. Following them came the mainguard in the following order:—Headquarters 3rd Infantry Brigade, Welch Regiment (less one Company and M.G. Section), Gloucesters, 26th Field Company R.E., South Wales Borderers, Queens, Brigade Reserve of S.A.A. carts (two carts per battalion) under Lieutenant Halford (28th), brigaded cookers and watercarts under Lieutenant Pain (Queens), and lastly the 43rd Brigade R.F.A.

The general scheme for the regimental transport in the first few days of the War was that the S.A.A. carts and the machine gun limbers, only, accompanied the battalions. Two S.A.A. carts per battalion were, however, taken away from units to form a Brigade S.A.A. Reserve. The rest of the Battalion 1st Line Transport (*i.e.*, tool carts, cookers and watercarts) were brigaded, whilst the supply and baggage wagons marched well to the rear with the Divisional Train.

The main road from Avesnes to Maubeuge and Mons was soon struck, and the fortified town of Maubeuge, about 7 miles to the north, was reached at 10 a.m. The town was found to be full of troops, busy completing the defences. These consisted of nine modern forts with intermediate fixed and mobile batteries. The whole perimeter was being surrounded by triple belts of wire, while the town itself was encircled by an old-time moat and ramparts, with the citadel in the centre. Soldiers and civilians were seen in all directions digging, cutting down trees, and generally preparing the town for any eventuality. The Brigade Group halted for the middle of the day in a cornfield just north of the town, near Fort des Sart, and at 3.15 p.m. marched off to a billeting area just south of the Belgian frontier. The Gloucesters proceeded to the village of Villers-sire-Nicole, immediately east of the main road leading to Mons. Here, after getting teas, the Battalion was suddenly turned out and ordered to dig trenches to the north of the village, as it was reported more German cavalry had been encountered about Bray, some 8 miles further north. At 6 p.m. fresh orders arrived, and General Landon's advanced guard was instructed to push on, to take up the line Peissant—Fauroeulx—Haulchin—Givry, and to hold it for the night. The Welch were ordered to occupy the right of the line about Peissant and Fauroeulx, the Gloucesters with the 26th Field Company about Haulchin, and the S.W.B. at Givry, where they were to join up with the 2nd Division near Havay. Brigade Headquarters, with the Queens in reserve, remained at Croix-lez-Rouveroy. The 43rd and 25th Brigades R.F.A. were to support the Welch and Gloucesters

22nd Aug. respectively, as required. On receipt of these orders, Colonel Lovett and the Company Commanders went forward to reconnoitre the frontage, while the Adjutant brought up the Battalion.

Haulchin was reached in the dark, about 10.30 p.m., and after outposts had been put out, the Battalion got into billets, after a long and fatiguing day, with its 22½ miles' march.

A portion of the 5th Cavalry Brigade, with their headquarters at Trieux, were out in front of the left flank of the 3rd Infantry Brigade, and connected up with the 2nd Division. This Division stretched north-west through Harmignies, whence the 3rd Division continued northwards to Obourg, and so along the canal encircling Mons itself, and as far as St. Ghislain. Further to the west lay the 5th Division and the 19th Infantry Brigade. Allenby's Cavalry Division was originally spread along the road from Mons as far east as Binche, to cover the I Corps. During the night, however, with the exception of the 5th Cavalry Brigade, it was withdrawn to the left of the British line. A small number of the 12th Lancers remained in Haulchin itself, and a quantity of their forage was discovered and appropriated in the dark for the Battalion, whose own forage had failed to arrive.

The early hours of the 23rd August were spent by the Regiment in hurriedly digging a line of entrenchments north and east of the village of Haulchin. Tools were commandeered from the inhabitants, and doors and shutters were taken to help make revetments and head cover. This resulted in most frightful scenes with the local population—one wonders what happened in the very near future, when the Huns poured over the same bit of country. Minor adjustments of the line occurred, but eventually a more or less continuous trench was constructed. D, C and B Companies, from right to left, were in the front line, whilst A Company was kept in support, with Battalion Headquarters in the village itself. General Lomax, commanding the 1st Division, inspected the Battalion's trenches the next day, and commented on the necessity of traverses as protection in the event of enfilade fire.

So secret had been the landing and moves of the British Army, that it was not until August 22nd that the German I Army had had any definite news as to its whereabouts; consequently, on the following day their first advance was more in the nature of a reconnaissance. The loop of the canal north of Mons was their first objective, but by noon the attack against the whole front of the II Corps became general. The 5th Cavalry Brigade, in advance of the I Corps, was forced to withdraw, and gradually the Germans, attacking in masses, succeeded in driving back the 3rd Division from the canal salient at Mons. The right wing of the II Corps was thus bent back, and more or less formed a continuation of the line of the I Corps, which had been somewhat echeloned to its rear.

At 5 p.m. Sir John French received an unexpected message from General Joffre, telling him that at least three German corps were moving against the British front, and that another was engaged in a turning movement further to the west, and finally that the Fifth French Army, on the right of the British Expeditionary Force, was retiring. This meant that against the British Force, whose strength was about 80,000 men, instead of about 130,000 Germans, there were 200,000 in the immediate front, about 45,000 sweeping round the left, and a victorious army pushing forward after the French on the right flank. As a result of this alarming information, Sir John French decided to withdraw at daybreak of the 24th to a reconnoitred position extending from Maubeuge, on the east, through Bavai, to Jenlain. A certain amount of fighting took place during the night, and at dawn on the 24th the 2nd Division made a demonstration in the neighbourhood of Harmignies, under cover of which the II Corps commenced to retire. Meanwhile further to the right arrangements for the withdrawal were being carried out.

In the Haulchin locality a few shots had been fired on the 23rd in the direction of C Company's trenches, apparently from a German cavalry patrol. No damage, however, was done. In the evening, and throughout the night, the shelling and bursts of rifle and machine gun fire could be heard away on the left front, and searchlights were seen, together with the glow of burning farms and hamlets. The general feeling at the time was how much more safe one would be if the battle could start in the morning, and not now, when it was just getting dark. The thoughts of an attack by night were much more terrifying—whereas by day everyone was confident of being able to withstand any hostile attack.

24th Aug.

Originally, at 3 a.m. on the 24th, the Gloucesters were ordered to hold their positions at all costs, and preparations were made to have ammunition, water and food up in the trenches. At 5 a.m. the transport was sent off to Croix-lez-Rouveroy, and the Battalion was ordered to be ready to retire at short notice. The 1st Brigade (less the Coldstream Guards) had been moved forward, and were occupying the position Villers-sire-Nicole—Bonnet, while the Queens, of the 3rd Brigade, together with the Coldstreamers, held a line between Croix and Rouveroy. At about 6.30 a.m. the Welch and S.W.B. were ordered to withdraw, and acting in conjunction, to retire to the line Noire Bouteille—Rouveroy. At the same time the Gloucesters were ordered to hold on at Haulchin, and to retire in conjunction with the 6th Brigade (2nd Division), who were about Vellereille-le-Sec. The Battalion was particularly instructed to hold on until word was received either from the 3rd Brigade or from General Davies, commanding the 6th Brigade, and then to withdraw in a south-westerly direction towards Bettignies. From their position about the cross roads north of Haulchin a most excellent view was obtained for about two thousand yards to the north, and soon after dawn on this morning the Battalion had its first opportunity of watching troops in action, and of seeing the effects of the enemy's shells bursting not too far away on the left front. A certain number of casualties were inflicted on the K.R.R., of the 6th Brigade, and the wounded were brought back through Haulchin.

At 7.10 a.m. a hastily written and almost illegible message arrived from 3rd Brigade: "Commence your retirement and get clear of Haulchin and behind Rouveroy—Givry line as soon as possible." The K.R.R., on the immediate left of the Battalion, had already withdrawn, and the Gloucesters only just got away in time without casualties. Their position was shelled directly they had left, and a cavalry patrol retiring in the valley to the north-west also came in for a shelling. Enemy cavalry could be seen in the distance, and one always wonders why their horse gunners never opened fire on what must have been an ideal target.

The Battalion had been ordered to retire, when necessary, across country parallel to the Binche—Bavai road. As, however, all the transport had not been got away in front, it was decided to march *via* Croix-lez-Rouveroy, where the Queens were known to have taken up a rearguard position. As soon as the rear party of the Battalion had got through the Queens' lines, a German cavalry patrol of six men came up to within 500 yards of the trenches. The Queens opened fire, and five of the patrol were knocked over, only the sixth man escaping. Another small incident worth noting also took place about this time. One of the Companies' issue of meat fell off the cooker whilst bumping across the open country. Although the enemy were really quite close, the cooks calmly took off their coats and set to work to reload and secure their day's rations on to the carts—and fortunately got away without any further troubles.

B Company, who had been on the left of the Battalion's position, retired parallel to the Bavai road, according to the first instructions, and got detached from the rest of the Regiment. They were shelled on the way, but proceeded across country in artillery formation, and did not suffer any casualties. The alteration in the route had not reached this Company when the sudden orders to retire came through. Captain Shipway, therefore, went off to get instructions. Whilst he was away, owing to a misunderstanding, two of the platoons of the Company, continuing to retire along the original line, again got separated, and for a short time were attached to the Loyal North Lancashire Regiment, holding Le Bonnet. They had a somewhat lucky escape from being surrounded by the enemy, and eventually caught up with the Battalion transport, near

24th Aug. Feignies, and rejoined in the evening. The rest of B Company joined up at Bettignies, after it had passed through the line being prepared by the 1st Brigade.

The 3rd Brigade was assembled at Bettignies, and resumed its march at about 5.40 p.m., *via* Gognies Chaussee—les Bas Vents—Feignies to Neuf Mesnil, around which it was to billet, just within the perimeter of the fortress of Maubeuge. The total march of the Gloucesters for the day amounted to 17 miles.

To cover the withdrawal of the I Corps, Sir Horace Smith-Dorrien had halted his force on the line Dour—Quarouble, and in his turn, when hard pressed, was covered by the cavalry and the 19th Infantry Brigade. At nightfall the whole of the British Army was in a position east and west of Bavai, with their right protected by the fortress of Maubeuge. The Fifth French Army, to the east of the town, had, however, again been driven back, and were once more retiring.

Thus finished the Battle of Mons, where the Army had withstood the attacks of an overwhelming number of the enemy, and although vigorously pursued at the commencement were able to pass victorious through all the trials and fatigues of the now famous Retreat from Mons.

The retirement was recommenced in the early morning of the 25th, to a position at Landrecies—Le Cateau—Cambrai, partially prepared by the 4th Division, which had newly arrived from England, and had detrained at Le Cateau on the 23rd.

Owing to the presence of the Foret de Mormal, the I Corps had to leave the immediate right flank of the II Corps, and to take a longer and more roundabout route to the east of the forest. The 1st Division had orders to move to the Noyelles—Landrecies area at the southern extremity of the forest.

The 3rd Brigade left their billets at Neuf Mesnil at about 4.30 a.m., and, preceded by one company of the Queens, with the Train of the Brigade Group, marched south in the following order:—26th Field Company, Queens, S.W.B., Welch, Gloucesters. The route taken was through Hautmont—Limont Fontaine—Monceau—Dompierre—Marbaix to Le Grand Fayt. Little was it thought only five days previously that parts of this same road would be used again, and in the opposite direction.

For the Brigade the march was uneventful, though most trying in the intense and glaring heat, and being, as it was, mostly along narrow country lanes. A halt was made at Marbaix, where dinners were prepared, and where a second mail from England was received. A storm at this time somewhat cooled the atmosphere, but when the march was continued, at about 5.30 p.m., it was still exceedingly hot, and the troops were exhausted when they arrived at Le Grand Fayt, although the distance covered did not exceed 15½ miles.

The 2nd Division this day had retired down the main Maubeuge—Landrecies road, but by the evening were still spread out from Landrecies to Leval.

About half an hour after the arrival at Le Grand Fayt, the alarm was given by a gunner major who galloped up from the west, followed by several heavy wagons tearing down the road at breakneck speed. He stated he had been surprised, and that his convoy had nearly been surrounded. The Gloucesters, who got this news first, immediately stood to arms, and advanced in extended order to the north-west outskirts of the village. It was found, however, there was no prospect of an immediate attack, and the Brigade thankfully turned in once more for a short night's rest.

C Company formed part of the outpost screen protecting the village, and throughout most of the night could hear machine gun and rifle fire comparatively close at hand. At times they could even distinctly hear cheering. The 4th Guards Brigade at Landrecies and the 6th Brigade at Maroilles were both attacked during the night by German detachments arriving through the Foret de Mormal from the north-west. At daybreak on the 26th the German I Army continued to bring pressure to bear on the British II Corps further to the west, and Sir Horace Smith-Dorrien judged it impossible to continue his retirement in the face of the expected attack. As a result the Battle of Le Cateau was fought, and although serious losses were incurred, the left wing of the British Army was able to break off the engagement at about 3.30 p.m. and, covered by the cavalry and artillery, the retreat was continued far into the night. **26th Aug.**

For the Gloucesters reveille was at 1 a.m. on the 26th August, but there was considerable delay before a move was made. Owing to the strain on the men having to carry such great weights for miles at a stretch, arrangements were made for all greatcoats and packs to be collected and taken away by lorries—presumably to the Base. They certainly went off in the early hours of the morning, but were never again seen by the men. Rumour had it that they were captured by the enemy. A new issue was not made until considerably later, when the Battalion was entrenched on the Aisne.

At about 4.30 a.m. the Battalion (less C and D Companies), acting as advanced guard to the Brigade moved out west towards Favril. The 39th Brigade R.F.A. and the 26th Field Company R.E., accompanied the column, while the 1st Line Transport not actually required by units turned south, and was directed to proceed *via* Prisches to Etreux. The previous night had been one of the few occasions when it was impossible for rations to be issued to the Brigade. All that could be done was to dump all the supplies at the side of the road for the men to snatch at for themselves as they passed the following morning.

On approaching Favril the two leading Companies of the Battalion were extended in a fan-like formation, B Company on the right of the road, and A Company on the left. The advance was continued through and beyond the village, and north-west along the road to Landrecies. Behind this screen the Brigade Commander carried out a rapid reconnaissance, and at 7.30 a.m. issued orders for the Brigade to occupy the line Fm de la Boufflette—Saule Bryante—Sambreton, in order to oppose the enemy's advance as he emerged from the southern exits of Landrecies. Very little was known of the general situation, or even where the remainder of the I Corps was. The 5th and 6th Brigades of the 2nd Division were believed to be fighting on the line Noyelles—Maroilles, some three or four miles to the north-east. The 4th Brigade, after its fight in the town of Landrecies of the previous night, was retiring south, and had just passed Sambreton. The rest of the 1st Division, after billeting for the night at Taisnieres and Marbaix, away on the east flank, were falling back in a south-westerly direction. The 3rd Infantry Brigade was carrying out the rearguard duties for the Division.

The South Wales Borderers were ordered to send one company to Fm de la Boufflette with a post thrown back to guard their right flank, while the rest of the battalion was held in reserve just north of Favril. The Gloucesters were to occupy the line from Fm de la Boufflette across the Favril—Landrecies road towards Sambreton ; while the Queens continued the line westwards across the Landrecies—La Groize road about Mon Rouge, with one company pushed forward to support the left of the Gloucesters. The Welch Regiment were kept in reserve at Favril.

With B Company thrown out in front almost to Faubourg de France as a protective screen, the Battalion entrenched a position behind the hedges on a slight rise to cover as far as possible the exits from Landrecies. C Company held to the right of the road, with its right slightly echeloned to the rear. In their trenches, and just off the road, was dug-in a section of the 54th Battery R.F.A., under Lieutenant Blewitt. On the west of the road was D Company and the machine gun section. A Company was withdrawn from its original forward position, and was held in reserve about 200 yards up the road towards Favril.

The country in front was very enclosed, much resembling the outskirts of a prosperous village in Kent. Accordingly it was hard to find any position where one could get a field of fire for more than the breadth of the field in front—about a couple of hundred yards at the most. B Company was about 500 yards in front of the main position, and occupied shallow rifle pits scooped out by entrenching tools in the ditches behind the hedgerows.

26th Aug. About noon it was reported that a column was moving east to west by a road north of Landrecies, about 2,000 yards away. It was uncertain if it was hostile or not, owing to difficulties of observation: only the heads and shoulders of mounted men could be seen. Soon after 1 p.m. a second column, with transport, was seen to be passing the same point. This time Lieutenant Blewitt opened fire with his guns, and appeared to do good shooting. The men scattered, and two shells burst right over a party of about 40 dismounted men before they could disperse. The enemy soon replied by shelling the spot occupied by the guns. The majority of their shots, however, burst in the fields, short of C Company, and did little damage, only creating some excitement amongst a herd of cattle. One or two men of the Company were wounded, and a pack animal was killed. Soon after this incident an aeroplane bearing the French colours flew over from the north. It was only a few hundred feet up, and was apparently under a heavy machine gun fire from the enemy. It appeared to nose-dive directly above the Regiment, and then righting itself, and flying along the whole length of the trenches, disappeared safely towards the north-east. Immediately after this the Germans got the exact range of the trenches and the road, and did a certain amount of damage. This story speaks for itself. It was the first example of the Huns' treachery that the Battalion had come across, and it was hard to be able to lower oneself to their level to be prepared for the next ruse. German infantry now also began to be felt, though, on account of the hedges and trees, very little of their movements could be seen. Most of their shots were fired from the left flank, and these, enfilading B Company's position, forced this Company to withdraw round the flanks to the rear of the main line. This movement was not, unfortunately, carried out without casualties. Captain Shipway himself was mortally wounded by a sniper, firing from a house in front. He was at the time out in front of his Company with C.Q.M.S. Brain, and a few others, trying to locate the enemy, in order to send back information. He was brought back and taken to Etreux by the Field Ambulance, but died there that same evening.

Private Lander, a fine old soldier of B Company, distinguished himself at this period. Although wounded, he continued firing, and accounted for three Germans before he was finally bayoneted to death. He was buried the next day by a party of the 4th Field Ambulance which had been left behind in Landrecies in charge of some 170 wounded men of the Guards Brigade who could not be removed in the ambulances. The burial service was read by the 4th Brigade padre, the Rev. O'Rourke, who previously had been serving at Bordon, with the 3rd Brigade. He, together with his servant, Private Whyman, of the Gloucesters, had returned to the village early on the 26th to do what he could for the wounded Guardsmen, and was taken prisoner with the rest of the party. Private Whyman was another old B Company soldier who had been left behind in England, as it was feared the strain of active service would be too much for his years. Before the War he had been servant to the Rev. O'Rourke, and when the latter was attached on the outbreak of the War to the Guards Brigade, he volunteered to accompany him as servant and groom.

A R.A.M.C. captain who had also been left behind in Landrecies, when describing the happenings of the day some years later, mentioned the incident of the " French " aeroplane, and said they could not make out what the Germans were shelling, as they had no idea there were any British troops in any numbers in the vicinity. He had seen, however, a party of about half-a-dozen men of the Gloucestershire Regiment strung out along the road to the south of the town, and who appeared to be lost. This must have been a patrol of four men under Sergeant Walsh, of A Company, which had been sent out to reconnoitre the outskirts of Landrecies. The patrol failed to return, and it was learnt later that the party, losing its way, eventually found itself in rear of the German lines. The men then split up with the idea of trying to break through to rejoin the Regiment. Sergeant Walsh and Private Habberfield got as far as Prisches (about four miles south-east of Landrecies), when they were cut off, Habberfield killed and Sergeant Walsh captured. The remainder were also eventually taken prisoners.

By about 5 p.m. in the afternoon the action between Landrecies and 26th Aug.
Favril had come to an end. The Germans did not seem at all anxious to
approach the main position occupied by the 3rd Brigade, and covered by the 39th Brigade
R.F.A., and the British rearguard was able to retire south through another position
prepared and held by the 1st and 2nd Brigades at Erruart—La Groise—Catillon. The
Brigade assembled at Petit Cambresis, and went into bivouac with practically the whole
of the 1st Division about Oisy. The German columns marching across the front of
the Battalion proved to be a portion of the German IX Corps. Von Kluck himself
also passed through Landrecies in the evening.

The Battalion had a most trying march back to Oisy. After a halt near La Groise
the last stage was made along the main Landrecies—Guise road, which at the time was
packed with troops. The centre of the road was occupied by artillery and transport;
the left had to be kept clear for cavalry and cyclists, who were continually passing up
and down, while the wretched infantry had to get along as best they could in the dark
and rain in the gutter on the right of the roadway. Oisy was, however, reached at about
10 p.m., and while the men got some dry straw to lie on, the officers found their valises
awaiting them for the first time since the march north began. The total distance of
the day's march was 15 miles. The casualties for the day, besides Captain Shipway,
amounted to 36, 5 killed, 21 wounded, 8 missing or prisoners, and 2 sick. Three pack
animals which had been up with the 1st Line Transport on the road behind the Battalion's
trenches had also been wounded.

As has been mentioned, the II Corps, after the fighting at Le Cateau, retired south-
west during the afternoon, roughly to the line Estrees—Vermand—Hargicourt. Luckily,
Von Kluck, believing the British Army would continue its retirement south-west, and
not wishing to change his direction at this stage, and so bring his I Army into the zone
allotted to Von Bülow's II Army, and, incidentally, to allow hostile forces to assemble
undisturbed on his right flank, failed to pursue French's weary troops with any vigour,
and the " Contemptible little army " of Britain was allowed for the greater part to
continue its retreat without being seriously hindered.

On August 27th the 1st Division followed the 2nd Division along the Guise road.
The 2nd Brigade formed a right flank guard, and proceeded through Wassigny. The 1st
Brigade Group formed the rear guard for the day. There was still a gap between the
two corps. The 3rd Brigade followed behind the Divisional Train, and was on the road
at about 10 a.m. After the first mile or so the Brigade closed up, and marched for some
distance two battalions abreast. The Gloucesters and South Wales Borderers marched
side by side at the head of the column. The object of this was apparently to deceive
hostile aircraft, and to economise in road space. After passing through Etreux, the
battalions were once more opened out, and there were many checks before Guise was
reached. After passing through this town, news came that the 1st Brigade had been
roughly handled on rearguard duty. The 3rd Brigade was accordingly turned about
to render what assistance it could. However, by the time it got very far out to the north
of Guise again, it was found the 1st Brigade had got clear of the enemy, though with the
loss of the Munster Fusiliers. The despatch rider conveying orders for this battalion to
retire was captured, and the regiment was surrounded. With the exception of some 150
men who escaped with the aid of the 15th Hussars, all were either killed or captured.
The Black Watch also nearly suffered the same fate further south, near Etreux, but
luckily just slipped away in time.

The 3rd Brigade turned south through Guise once more, and branching south-west
along the St. Quentin road, proceeded some five miles, when it turned west along small
lanes, and crossed the River Oise at Bernot, where it was billeted for the night. There
was very little room in the village, but the troops were only too glad to turn in anywhere,
after a long march of 23 miles. The regimental transport had arrived earlier in the
evening, and had been ordered to put out outposts, and to construct street barricades.

27th Aug. These, on the arrival of the Battalion, were taken over by the Machine Gun Section, which remained on duty throughout the night, protecting the northern approaches to the village.

The difference at Guise when the Brigade passed through for the second time was most marked. The first time the townspeople were carrying on their daily occupations, and the place was comparatively full. The second time, however, the town itself was almost deserted. Shops and houses were all shut up, and everyone was hurrying off south and east in all manner of vehicles. A battalion of Alpins Chasseurs was in the town, but all other men of military age were being marched off to join the Colours.

During the day the following message of congratulation was received by the Battalion from the Brigade Commander :—

"I am intensely proud of the courageous spirit and stubborn endurance with which all Battalions of the 3rd Brigade have faced the severe trial of the past 14 days. The already famous Battalions composing the Brigade have nobly added to their past history by their recent deeds, and this knowledge should brace them to face a continuance, if necessary, and to renewed efforts towards the final defeat of the enemy. I am sure everyone knows how greatly I have felt for them in the hardships endured, and how deeply I deplore the loss of so many gallant comrades of all ranks."

It was not until the 29th that an opportunity occurred for this letter to be read out to the various Companies.

In place of Captain Shipway, Captain Blunt was transferred from A Company to command B Company.

On the 28th August hostile columns were reported to be approaching St. Quentin. The 3rd and 5th Cavalry Brigades were operating between this town and the right rear of the I Corps. The retreat was to be continued this day, and the 2nd Brigade, which formed the rearguard, was ordered to be in position from Jonquese to north of Hautville by 4 a.m. Of the 3rd Brigade, the Queens were ordered to establish two Companies, with the remainder in reserve, on the heights north of Bernot, to deny them to hostile artillery. They were to remain in position until directed by General Bulfin, commanding the rearguard, to withdraw. The rest of the Brigade, preceded by its 1st Line Transport, was to continue the retreat along the eastern bank of the River Oise, towards La Fere. Reveille was at what became to be the usual hour—5 a.m.,—and the Battalion was on the road at 7.30 a.m. The Gloucesters, however, were not all to march with the Brigade, for two companies—A and C—were detailed to act as a right flank guard, and to march south along the ridge on the west bank of the river. During the morning they succeeded in capturing two German spies, who were given away whilst working in the fields by the inhabitants.

B and D Companies, under Major Ingram, followed the Brigade, and passing through Neauvillette, crossed once more to the east of the Oise, and proceeded through Mont Origny, where the greater part of the 2nd Division had billeted the previous night, and where preparations for a stand against the enemy were being made.

The column halted for several hours in the middle of the day in an orchard near Sery-les-Mezieres. Here a welcome wash was possible in a stream. Although there was very little depth, and most of that was dirty and very muddy, it enabled all ranks to get the first real wash since they had left Havre, nearly a fortnight before.

The rest of the Battalion rejoined in the afternoon, and at about 5 p.m. the march was continued along the Oise valley, as far as the old fortified town of La Fere. Here the Brigade branched south-east along the main Laon road, and marched into billets and bivouacs about Bertaucourt, after doing 21 miles during the day.

The 4th Guards Brigade were occupying the western part of the village, while the 2nd Brigade were billeted about Fressaucourt, to the north-east. The 3rd Brigade were ordered to block and piquet the various roads to the north and north-east of **29th Aug.** Bertaucourt, whilst the 4th Brigade did the same to the north-west.

To the Gloucesters was allotted a large chateau, with good outbuildings, in which most of the men got accommodation. The remainder secured straw, and were comparatively comfortable in the orchard and under walls.

August 29th was spent as a rest day—or rather, the situation did not call for the I Corps to retire any further south for 24 hours, partly because the German pursuit had for some reason somewhat slackened. There was, however, very little real rest, as apart from the general cleaning up and overhauling of arms and kit, etc., so essential after the last two weeks of incessant marching and fighting, the chateau grounds had to be put into some state of defence. The walls surrounding the place were loopholed, and the various companies given tasks to carry out in the defence. Later in the day, the Gloucesters were required to make secure the northern and north-eastern approaches to the Brigade bivouac. Companies, in turn, were then ordered out to construct trenches on a slight rise outside the grounds, to cover the open country towards La Fere, and also to barricade the roads. La Fere itself was occupied at the time by British and French troops, and the 5th Cavalry Brigade had parties north of the River Oise.

The Brigade Commander, when visiting the Battalion during the day, expressed his approval at the digging done, and again complimented the Regiment on its fine work of the past days. The following message was also received from the Navy during the day through Lord Kitchener :—

" First Lord asks me to transmit to you the following message from the Home Fleet : ' The officers and men of the Grand Fleet wish to express to their comrades of the Army, admiration of the magnificent stand made against great odds, and wish them the brilliant success which the Fleet feels sure awaits their further efforts.' "

Permission was given on the 29th to those units whose S.A.A. carts were not full to relieve the men by taking their spare ammunition up to the carts' full capacity. No man was, however, to carry less than 150 rounds, the weight of which, on a long day's march, can well be imagined.

It appears that the original destination of the Battalion for the night of the 28th/29th was to have been Barisis au Foret. When the Battalion, with the rest of the 3rd Brigade, was diverted towards Bertaucourt, the 1st Line Transport found itself cut off, and without knowledge of where to join the Battalion. After a most trying night march along tracks through the forest, they reached Barisis, when it was discovered where the regiments were billeting. As a result of all this, Lieutenant Halford was not able to rejoin the Battalion until about midday of the 29th, when the horses could be outspanned for the first time for three days.

An alteration was made at this period as regards the regimental transport. In the future the cookers and watercarts were ordered to join the Train, instead of forming part of the 1st Line. The watercart was to be drawn by one horse only, and the second animal was to be taken on by battalions as a spare.

Mention may also be made at this point of the cold-shoer—Private Green,—who kept all the animals going during the retreat. He was continually to be seen at work during the ten minutes' halts at the side of the road. He must have reshod every horse before the Aisne was reached.

The transport was repacked at 6 o'clock in the evening of the 29th, in readiness to move southwards, and it actually proceeded through the Foret de St. Gobain, just before midnight, well before the infantry were on the roads again. At 7.30 p.m. B Company was ordered out to take up an outpost line about half a mile outside the chateau, and to get in touch with the Brigades on the flanks. There was a considerable amount of firing on the left, in front of the Scots Guards, but no troubles in the sector allotted to the Battalion.

30th Aug. During the 29th the two Commanders-in-Chief had held a conference, when it was arranged to carry out anyhow a further short retirement to the Aisne, while the new French Sixth Army was being rapidly formed on the Allied left flank.

About half an hour after midnight, preliminary orders were received to the effect that owing to a reverse of the French about Mezieres and Sedan, the I Army Corps would continue its march south. The 3rd Brigade, together with the 39th Brigade R.F.A., the 26th Field Company, and the Bearer sub-division, 3rd Field Ambulance, would act as rearguard to the 1st Division. Troops were to be ready to move at 4.30 a.m., August 30th. The Gloucesters this day formed the rear party to the Brigade. The morning was exceedingly foggy, and as all the companies proceeded by side roads and lanes over the heights and through the St. Gobain Forest, the first part of the march was exceptionally slow, and there were continuous checks in order that communication might be kept up between units.

Battalion Headquarters and B Company (the latter in reserve after the night on outpost duty) proceeded *via* St. Gobain, Septvaux and Premontre. The Brigade Group arrived at Brancourt in the early afternoon, after a short (10 miles) but hot march, with considerable climbing.

On Monday, 31st, the retreat was continued south-west. The Brigade started off at about 6 a.m., through Pinon, which was full of French motor and horse transport, and Allemant, where a portion of the 1st Division had bivouacked the previous night. The main road from Laon was then followed down through the chalk hills to the valley of the Aisne, and the river was crossed at Soissons. It was hoped that the Division would halt for the night near the town, but instead they continued south for another 4 miles, up a very steep hill to Missy-aux-Bois, on the Villers-Cotterets road. This proved to be a bad bivouac, as it was close to the dusty road, and far from water and fuel. Carrying parties had to go a mile for these necessities. The total distance of the day's march was 18 miles. The Train with the officers' valises was once more handy, but the men suffered somewhat during the night from cold without their greatcoats.

September 1st was a day of hard fighting in the woods of Compiegne and Villers-Cotterets. The 4th Guards Brigade was forced to fight a sharp rearguard action on the northern edge of the latter forest, and the 1st Cavalry Brigade were nearly surprised and surrounded at Nery.

The Gloucesters commenced their march at 6 a.m., and proceeded along the straight road to Villers-Cotterets. Here a halt was made for dinners. The River Ourcq was crossed at La Ferte-Millon, and the Brigade arrived at Mareuil-sur-Ourcq, where it was to bivouac, at 3 o'clock in the afternoon. Lieutenant Caunter was forced to fall out sick during this march, and was sent down to a base hospital. The day was uneventful throughout for the Regiment. The length of the march was 19 miles.

A platoon of B Company was sent out to piquet the road going east to Dammard. Their chief duty was to turn back parties of refugees who were now encumbering the roads with their columns of country carts and wagons full of the aged and infirm and their household treasures. It was a pitiful sight to see all these hundreds of homeless families, untended and almost uncared for, in those days of anxiety. Except for those too old to serve in the army, and one or two priests, there were no men to help them along, and it is feared many had a more terrible time than if they had remained in their homes.

A very early start was made during the night of the 1st/2nd September. The 2nd Brigade were detailed to form the rearguard for the march. They commenced to retire first, in order to hold positions at Varinfroy and Le Plessis-Placy, to cover the rest of the Division. The 3rd Brigade in the following order :—South Wales Borderers, Welch, Gloucesters, Queens, 39th Brigade R.F.A., Bearers 3rd Field Ambulance, marched at the head of the Division, and started south along the main road to Meaux at 1.30 a.m. The leading battalion, the South Wales Borderers, were ordered to piquet all the roads leading

to the east, and to rejoin the column in front of the rearguard when it passed.   2nd Sept.
Miles of up and down country were covered in the dark. Once a halt was made, and the Brigade expected to take up a position of defence; nothing, however, came of it, and the retirement was continued well into the heat of the day. There had again been no opportunity of issuing rations or of filling waterbottles before the march started. Later in the morning water was luckily obtainable whilst passing through a village, and during a halt at about midday a limited number of tins of bully beef were distributed for dinner from the emergency " iron " rations.

About 1½ miles north of Meaux the 3rd Brigade turned west to Cregy, where billets were procured. The march of the day was 18½ miles, but owing to marching so much in the dark, the distance seemed considerably more.

September 3rd was spent for the most part in getting the British Army over the River Marne, with a view to defending the passages over the river as long as possible, and then to destroy the bridges It was necessary at this stage for the right flank of the B.E.F. to extend further to the east, to connect up with the Fifth French Army.

Orders were received at 1.30 a.m. for an immediate move, and by 2.30 a.m. the Brigade was on the road once more. The order of march for the day was the Queens in front, followed by the Welch, Gloucesters, and lastly the South Wales Borderers. The 1st Division was eventually to march *via* La Ferté to Coulommiers, but the 3rd Brigade started south through Meaux, and then turned north, and up the road used the previous day, as far as Varreddes. Here the River Marne was crossed, and the route then taken was almost due east, along the south bank of the river. At about midday a halt was made near St. Jean, where dinners were prepared, and where the third mail from England joined the Battalion. Whilst at this spot a message was received that the Germans had been seen on the high ground across the river to the north-east. As a result, the column started off again in its easterly direction. Just short of La Ferté-sous-Jouarre, leaving the 2nd Brigade to guard two bridges over the river, the 3rd Brigade wheeled to the south, to Signy-Signets, where they halted for the night. A distance of 16½ miles was covered during the day. The Welch and South Wales Borderers were lucky, and were billeted in Perreuse Chateau, while the Gloucesters and Queens had to bivouac near-by, beside a large lake.

The British Army this night stretched from this point, near Signy-Signets, as far west as Lagny—within easy shell-fire from the forts of Paris.

After the necessary dispositions and demolitions had been effected, Sir John French was asked once more to continue the retirement—this time to a point about 12 miles in rear of the position then occupied, with a view to taking up a further position behind the Seine. On the following morning, therefore, the Army was on the move once more. It was now found that the pursuit of the enemy was becoming more vigorous. Von Kluck's I Army, which had been steadily advancing south-west, commenced on the 30th August to swing round, and to continue on a line slightly to the east of south. Up to the 3rd September, Von Bülow's II Army, which should have been pressing the British Army, was far too busy with the Fifth French Army to worry much with the British, who had been " practically annihilated at Le Cateau." On the 29th August this French Army had actually advanced to the attack, instead of retiring. By doing so, however, they had attracted the attention of Von Kluck, who thought they had at last come within his grasp, and could be enveloped.

During the 4th September the Germans were busy in crossing the Marne by means of temporary bridges which they had hastily thrown across.

The 3rd Brigade commenced to withdraw further south at about 5 a.m., proceeding in the following order:—39th Brigade R.F.A., South Wales Borderers, Queen, Gloucesters, and Welch. The first part of the march was across country, in order to strike the main La Ferté—Coulommiers road. Shortly after starting the Battalion, with the Welch behind, lost touch with the Queens owing to the mist. They, however, joined up with

5th Sept. the Brigade again at Mouroux, about 1½ miles west of Coulommiers. This village, where it was expected to remain for the night, was reached about 11 a.m., after a march of 11½ miles. There was practically no billeting accommodation, and the last two battalions to arrive had to bivouac in the orchards, and were ordered to remain under cover of the trees, to keep concealed from hostile aircraft.

After dinners, B and C Companies and the Machine Gun Section, under Major Ingram, were ordered off to the high ground near Bois la Ville, north of Mouroux, to dig a line of trenches to fill a gap between the 2nd Division, whose right was at Giremoutiers, and the 2nd Brigade, about Aulnoy. C Company put Bois la Ville in a state of defence, while B Company entrenched along the slight ridge to the east. The 2nd Brigade, on the right, were shelled during the afternoon, but otherwise there were no signs of the enemy. A patrol of three men of B Company got lost in the evening, and eventually wandered back through C Company's area. One of the machine guns opened fire on them, but no damage was done.

At about 6.15 p.m. the Brigade moved further south, to bivouac on the high ground about Limosin, about a mile from Coulommiers. The half battalion of the Gloucesters on outpost duty were put under the command of the officer commanding the 1st Black Watch, of the 1st Brigade. This battalion was on the same duty to the immediate north of Coulommiers, and on the right of Major Ingram's detachment.

Very early the following morning the 2nd Division, further to the west, commenced to retire towards Chaumes. At about 2 a.m. the 2nd Brigade, who were to find the advanced guard for the day, started to move south through Coulommiers, followed by the 1st Brigade. The Black Watch and the Gloucester companies were ordered to hold on to their positions until the whole of the 1st Division had got clear of the town. This they did, and it was not until about 4 a.m. that B and C Companies marched south to rejoin the Battalion. The 3rd Brigade had been detailed for rearguard duty for this day, and were standing to arms on the high ground south of Coulommiers, to cover the retirement of the other two brigades.

At 6.15 a.m. the Brigade marched south-west, through Mauperthuis. Between Rigny and Ormeau a longish halt was made for a meal under cover of outposts found by the Welch Regiment. On resuming the march, the Battalion proceeded across country, while the transport went round by road. The cross-country journeys of the previous days had proved somewhat disastrous for the regimental transport. The poles of the rear half of the machine gun cart and of one of the cookers had broken.

Rozoy-en-Brie, where the Brigade was to bivouac was reached soon after 3 o'clock in the afternoon, after a 15-mile march. It was D Company's turn to find that portion of the outposts allotted to the Battalion. They occupied a position across the road from Voinsles and Raperie, and connected up with the Queens on their right, and the 1st Brigade on their left. During the night parties of the enemy bumped up against the British east of Rozoy, but were caught by the artillery, and suffered considerably.

In the evening of the 5th, the Base Details, consisting of 93 men, under Captain A. A. McLeod, joined the Battalion, and were posted to companies. Captain McLeod joined A Company.

The Battalion, on the arrival of this draft, was 937 men strong, or one captain, one subaltern, and thirty-three other ranks below war establishment. The newly-arrived draft had left Bordon on the 22nd August, and had reached Amiens two days later. The Advanced Base at this town was just at this time being evacuated, and all British troops transferred to Rouen and Le Mans. At both of these places the men were able to do a certain amount of training.

What was almost more welcome in the Battalion than these fresh men, was the small supply of new boots, socks and shirts. There were the first to be received since the departure from England, and as all second sets had to be left with the abandoned packs on August 26th, all ranks were badly in need of clean kit and fresh footwear.

Many of the boots had been worn right through, and were quite useless. **6th Sept.**
Socks, also, in several cases were absolutely lacking.

At midnight orders were received to continue the movement towards Guignes, but these instructions were cancelled a few hours later.

On September 6th, the retreat, which had last twelve days and nights, and during which the Regiment had marched exactly 200 miles, was changed into an advance, and the movement for the next days was to be in a northerly direction.

The following table shows the lengths of the daily marches during the Retreat from Mons as far as the Gloucesters were concerned :—

24th August	-	Haulchin to Neuf Mesnil	-	17 miles.
25th ,,	-	,, La Grand Fayt	-	15½ ,,
26th ,,	-	,, Oisy	-	15 ,,
27th ,,	-	,, Bernot	-	23 ,,
28th ,,	-	,, Bertaucourt	-	21 ,,
29th ,,	-	,, Bertaucourt	-	—
30th ,,	-	,, Brandcourt	-	10 ,,
31st ,,	-	,, Missy aux Bois	-	18 ,,
1st Sept.	-	,, Mareuil	-	19 ,,
2nd ,,	-	,, Cregy	-	18½ ,,
3rd ,,	-	,, Signy Signets	-	16½ ,,
4th ,,	-	,, Mouroux	-	11½ ,,
5th ,,	-	,, Rozoy	-	15 ,,

Total of 200 miles in 13 days, or an average of 15.4 miles a day. Previous to this there had also been the advance from the point of concentration northwards to Mons, which was an additional march of 44 miles :—

Date		To		Distance
20th August	-	-	to Beaurepaire	-	8½ miles
21st ,,	-	-	,, Dourlers	-	13 ,,
22nd ,,	-	-	,, Haulchin	-	22½ ,,

On the 5th September, General Joffre informed Sir John French that he intended to take the offensive forthwith. The German right wing was considered to be so far exposed to the newly-formed Sixth French Army, which held a north and south line to the west of the British Army, that a movement to roll up the enemy's outer flank was believed to be possible. This was the news that was able to be given out by the officers to their men on the morning of the 6th, and it can be imagined with what delight it was received by all ranks.

Von Kluck was, however, quick to see the trap into which he was being led, and rapidly reinforced his right flank, and Marwitz's II Cavalry Corps was left practically on its own to check the pursuit of the British Force. General French was asked to wheel his army about its right flank in such a manner as to face north-east, and so, with Conneau's French Cavalry Corps, to fill completely the gap between the Fifth and Sixth French Armies. Although the advance on the 6th was somewhat slow, by the evening the line of the Grand Morin was reached, and in some places an advance of 12 miles had been carried out. The 3rd Brigade, preceded by an advanced guard, marched off from Rozoy at 7.30 a.m. in a southerly direction to the village of Courpalay. Here a halt was ordered, and the Brigade was held in readiness to support the 1st Brigade, who were engaged to the north-west. The outposts of the previous night had been instructed to remain out until the 1st Brigade had arrived. D Company, therefore, did not rejoin the Battalion until about 10.30 a.m.

At about 4 p.m. in the afternoon the march was resumed, though interrupted by long halts. This time the column pushed on in a north-easterly direction. Between 6

6th Sept. and 9 o'clock, covered by outposts found by the Queens, the Brigade went into bivouac north-east of Vaudoy. The total distance covered by the Battalion this day was 10 miles. Next morning the three German cavalry divisions opposite to the B.E.F. were driven north, and the Grand Morin was crossed. The 3rd Brigade did not commence what was to be an uneventful march of 13½ miles until about midday. The morning was spent hanging about in the open under a blazing sun, which tired the men considerably before they started the march. A certain amount of amusement was, however, found in searching the locality of the bivouac, as it was discovered to have been the scene of a cavalry encounter on the previous day. Lances and saddle-bags, etc., were seized as trophies, only to be discarded when the march commenced.

The route taken was by Dagny and Chevru. Here, as another column was using the main road to Choisy, the 3rd Brigade continued *via* the Leudon road and cart tracks to a point just east of Choisy-en-Brie. This was not a good bivouac, as it was very exposed, and the only cover that could be obtained was from some very thistly corn. Neither was there any water supply near at hand. It had previously been used by the enemy also as a bivouac ground, and their rubbish, papers, bottles, etc., were still lying about. As the Brigade was on the extreme right of the British Army, the South Wales Borderers had been detailed during the day as a flank guard.

September 8th was spent forcing the passage of the Petit Morin, thereby considerably helping the French Fifth Army, which had been held up further to the east. There was a certain amount of opposition all along the line of the river. The 2nd Division was checked for a time about Le Tretoire, north of Rebais, while the 1st Brigade met with the enemy between Bellot and Sablonnieres.

The 3rd Brigade were on the road at 5.30 a.m., and proceeded through Choisy village north-west to La Ferté Gaucher, passing on the way German lorries and many abandoned rifles and stores. Order of march for the day was as follows:—Welch, one battery R.F.A., Gloucesters, Queens, South Wales Borderers, 39th Brigade R.F.A., brigaded cookers and watercarts, brigade S.A.A. reserve (two carts per battalion), 3rd Field Ambulance. At La Ferté Gaucher the 1st Reinforcements, under Captain A. Capel, joined the Battalion. These consisted of 90 reservists, who had left England on August 26th. They had trained up from St. Nazaire, which was now the British Base after the evacuation of Le Havre.

The halt at this place was also an opportunity for filling water-bottles, which could not be replenished at Choisy, owing to lack of water. At St. Bartelemy a number of French cavalry, in their gaudy blue and scarlet uniforms and breastplates, were passed. At about this time word came back concerning the holding up of the 1st Brigade near Bellot. Heavy firing was also heard further to the west, where the 2nd Division were crossing the Petit Morin. The 3rd Brigade were hurried forward, chiefly in artillery formation, straight across country to reinforce. On arrival at Sablonnieres, it was found that the 1st Brigade, assisted by the 1st Cavalry Brigade, had been able to force a crossing over the river. The advance was continued through Hondevilliers, and as far north as the main Montmirail—Meaux road. Here the Brigade halted for the night near the Ferme de l'Ile. The latter stage of the march had again been across country, and in the midst of a violent thunderstorm and drenching rain. The total march was 17 miles, but the tremendous gunfire which appeared to be waging on every side, and the expectations of a scrap with the enemy, kept everyone on the go, and keen to press on. The bivouac ground was reached just before it became dark, and there was time to collect shocks of corn to build protection against the wind, and to get large fires burning to try and dry the men's clothing. Fresh meat had been issued for the first time for very many days. Unfortunately, the heat had been too much for it; it all had to be thrown away, and resort made once more to tinned beef.

A Company was out on outposts during the night. Shortly after midnight one of their posts fired at a party of men moving across their front. This proved to be nine men of the Garde Jager, under an officer. They surrendered themselves, and appeared to be half famished, and very glad to be safe, after wandering about lost between the opposing armies. **9th Sept.**

On the 9th September the advance was again continued, and the River Marne crossed. The II Corps, in the centre, was able to push on well ahead, but the I Corps, on the right, was somewhat delayed owing to the threat of an attack from the direction of Chateau Thierry, which was still in the hands of the enemy. The III Corps, on the left, were also hung up, as the bridges over the river in their area had been destroyed. However, by the afternoon the British had successfully driven back Marwitz's cavalry, and were established on the general line of the Chateau Thierry—Lizy sur Ourcq road, covered by cavalry. The 3rd Brigade had been ordered to lead the 1st Division across the Marne at Nogent, and accordingly the Gloucesters, who were advanced guard for the day, left their bivouac at 5 a.m., and pushed through the woods to the high ground overlooking Nogent, the river valley and the woods and vineyards to the north. The cavalry had already crossed the river with very little opposition, and reported that the immediate vicinity was clear. The Brigade pushed on into Nogent l'Artaud, and crossed the river. Attempts had been made by the enemy to destroy the single bridge at this point, but after several hours' unsuccessful work, they had been forced to leave it. The town had been thoroughly looted by the Huns before they left. The doors all bore chalk marks denoting their billeting arrangements. Inside, through the doors and broken windows, could be seen all the rooms ransacked and upside down, and a liberal display of empty bottles.

On the opposite bank of the river, the 3rd Brigade turned west to Charly, and thence north once more, and ascended the further slopes. The advance was, however, being continually checked to enable the remainder of the I Corps to cross to the north bank of the Marne. A longish halt was made at midday near Ferme Beaurepaire, and it was nearly dark by the time the Battalion reached its bivouac, near a wood at Le Thiolet, on the main Chateau Thierry—Lizy road. The distance covered on the 9th was 13 miles, of which the greater part was across country or up the narrow lanes amongst the vineyards.

During the night another welcome supply of boots and socks, etc., arrived for distribution to the most needy.

By this time the Battle of the Marne had been won, and the German Army was in full retreat. After very severe fighting along the River Ourcq, further to the west the Sixth French Army, having been reinforced from Paris, had been just able to hold its own, while on the right of the Fifth French Army the newly-arrived Ninth Army, under Foch, was able gradually to force back and break the enemy line about La Fere—Champenoise.

On the following day, 10th September, there was, however, fighting throughout most of the day. Two thousand prisoners and 13 guns were taken by the B.E.F. alone.

At 9.30 a.m. the 3rd Brigade commenced their march, and followed in rear of the 2nd Brigade, who were the protective troops for the day. The route taken was through Torcy and Courchamp. From here shells were seen bursting over the high ground a few miles ahead, and on arrival at Priez it was found the 2nd Brigade, and in particular the Royal Sussex, had been heavily engaged with the German rearguards. General Findlay, C.R.A. 1st Division, had been killed in action near this village, which, even by the time the Battalion passed through, was being used by the various Field Ambulances. The 3rd Brigade, north of Priez, turned east to Sommelans, where they bivouacked right in the open on a very exposed portion of the country. On the way there was much evidence of the hasty retreat of the enemy; the sides of the roads were littered with their cow-hide equipment, ammunition, etc. Sommelans was reached at 6.30 p.m., after a march of 11 miles.

On 11th September the advance was continued with little opposition. The Brigade Group left its bivouac at about 5.30 a.m. and marched in rear of the 1st Brigade. The Battalion marched second in the column. The British front was somewhat narrowed

11th Sept. during the day, owing to the slight change of direction of certain French armies. The 1st Division marched in a north-easterly direction the whole day. The Regiment proceeded *via* Latilly—Grisolles—Rocourt St. Martin—Coiney to Villeneuve sur Fere, where it bivouacked once more in the open. The march was about 11½ miles long, and Villeneuve was reached soon after 2 p.m. The weather this day changed very suddenly for the worse. Heavy rain fell, the temperature dropped considerably and the lack of greatcoats was badly felt. An effort was made during the afternoon to get all the troops under cover. With the exception of A Company, for whom there was no accommodation, the Battalion was eventually crowded into the small farms near the village.

The 12th September is considered the first day of the Battle of the Aisne, which was to last about a month.

On the evening of the 11th the British cavalry had reached the valley of the Aisne, a little south of a line drawn from Soissons to Cerseuil. Fairly early on the next day it became apparent that the German retirement was, anyhow for the moment, stayed, and that the excellent defensive position of the river was to be stoutly held by the enemy. The Aisne at this point is about 60 yards in breadth, sluggish, but unfordable. On either bank first of all a flat stretch of land, varying from a half to one mile in width, then the wooded and downlike bluffs rising to a height of about 400 feet, overlooking the river itself and its crossings. These crossings, however, had all been destroyed to a certain degree, and were all under either direct or indirect artillery fire.

Saturday, 12th September, found the 3rd Brigade Group once more the advanced guard to the 1st Division. The 2nd Welch was in the vanguard, whilst the Gloucesters headed the main guard. The billets at Villeneuve were left at 5 a.m., and the march headed north-east, through Fere-en-Tardenois, Loupeigne and Bazoches. On nearing this latter village, information was received that the Germans were occupying the high ground north of the River Vesle about Perles. At about 1 p.m. the Welch Regiment was sent forward to reconnoitre, and the 28th was ordered to deploy, and to advance west of the road leading up the valley from Bazoches to Vauxcéré. A and B Companies were extended in the first line, with C and D Companies in support. No trace of the enemy was found. As, however, it was decided to rest the night about here, A and B Companies were left out on outposts west of " Point 157 " to the north of the village of Vauxcéré. Two companies of the Welch continued this line to the east, where the left of the Fifth French Army was joined. The French had advanced in close touch with the 3rd Brigade all the day, and one of their trains of motor buses had been passed in the village of Mont Notre Dame.

The weather during the day had continued very bad and the roads, especially the country lanes up the hills, were, owing to the rains and unusual amount of heavy traffic, in an exceedingly bad condition. The transport and artillery were continually sticking in the ruts and mud during the latter stages of the march, which, to add to the difficulties, ended in the dark.

The troops not on outpost were billeted mostly in caves in the village of Vauxcéré. These caverns in the limestone district of the Aisne were greatly used by both armies during the whole War, and especially in these days of early trench warfare, when it was discovered how essential it was to get below the surface of the ground, and out of reach of artillery fire. The distance covered by the Battalion on the 12th was about 18½ miles. Letters from England, dated 26th August, arrived during the day's march. The cold and wet were the cause at this time of a number of men going sick with dysentery and chills, and the ambulance wagons behind the columns were kept constantly full. On this day Lieutenants Harding and Grazebrook, both of B Company, were forced to leave the Battalion on account of sickness, though the former officer was able to rejoin after three days.

On the 13th September the actual crossing of the Aisne commenced. While the II and III Corps had difficulties owing to the destruction of the bridges, the I Corps, with the cavalry on their right, met with only slight resistance at the first, and **13th Sept.** the 1st Division was able to cross the river by the aqueduct which carries the canal over the Aisne near Bourg. The cavalry also crossed by this duct, and by a bridge further to the east of Villers. On the left two brigades of the 2nd Division crossed at Pont d'Arcy and Chavonne with great difficulty. The 1st Division was, however, able to push well on along the Laon road, and by night-time the leading brigade, the 1st, had reached Moulins, while the 2nd Brigade came up on their right and occupied a line stretching through Paissy and Geny. Further still to the east were the cavalry linking up with the French who had crossed the river east of Bourg. The 3rd Brigade, who were in reserve, did not leave Vauxcéré until the early afternoon, when it proceeded to cross the river by the canal aqueduct, and billeted for the night in Bourg et Comin.

The following table shows the distances covered by the Battalion on its march to the Aisne after the 6th September, when the B.E.F. commenced its pursuit of the German army :—

6th Sept. -	Rozoy to Vaudoy	-	- 10 miles.
7th ,, -	,, Choisy	-	- 13½ ,,
8th ,, -	,, Ferme de l'Ile	-	- 17 ,,
9th ,, -	,, Le Thiolet	-	- 13 ,,
10th ,, -	,, Sommelans	-	- 11 ,,
11th ,, -	,, Villeneuve	-	- 11½ ,,
12th ,, -	,, Vauxcéré	-	- 18½ ,,
13th ,, -	,, Bourg	-	- 5 ,,

This made the total to be 99½ miles in the eight days, and a grand total of 343½ miles in the 25 days, starting at 20th August, when the first billets at Leschelles were left.

The 14th September was a day of almost continual fighting along the whole 15-mile front occupied by the British Army. It was, however, on the extreme right that the greatest advance was made and it was largely owing to the capture of the high ground about Chivy and Troyon by the 1st Division that the rest of the British front towards Soissons was at all tenable for the ensuing weeks. With a view to clearing up the general situation, the I Corps had been given orders to cross the line Moulins—Moussy by 7 a.m., and to seize the crest line of the heights to the north of the River Aisne. From here, along the famous Chemin des Dames, the whole country to the north towards Laon lay in full view.

The movement of the 1st Division began before dawn. The 2nd Brigade advanced through Moulins and Troyon towards the Chemin des Dames. Just short of Cerny, and north of Troyon, at the five cross roads, stood a sugar factory, which was strongly held by the enemy. The road to the east, and the road leading south-west to Chivy, were also occupied for a distance of about a quarter of a mile on either side of the factory. This position proved too strong for the leading three battalions of the 2nd Brigade, and the Loyal North Lancashire Regiment was sent forward from brigade reserve to assist. At the same time, 6 a.m., the 1st Brigade was also called upon to take part in the attack on the German trenches along the ridge. With the exception of the Coldstream Guards, who went to the right, this brigade continued the line of the 2nd Brigade further to the west. The final attack, which resulted in the capture of the sugar factory by the L.N.L., was an exceptionally fine piece of work, especially when one considers how unfavourable were the conditions. Although the attackers were sheltered by the steeper slopes, when they appeared at the final glacis they were met with an almost overwhelming burst of close range fire from rifles and machine guns from the inverted crescent formation of the enemy's position, and from two batteries of artillery just in rear of the Chemin des Dames. The attackers had also to contend with a rain driving in their faces, and which made the clay fields, planted with beet, unspeakably heavy and exhausting to cross.

The 3rd Brigade, which had spent the previous night in Bourg, commenced their march north along the road to Vendresse at 7.30 a.m. For the first two miles the progress

14th Sept. was very slow, heavy firing was heard just in front, but everyone was ignorant of what was actually taking place. About 9.30 a.m., just before Vendresse was reached, the Queens were sent to occupy the Paissy ridge, to protect the right rear of the Division. The remainder of the Brigade was then hurried forward through the village, and then north-west to extend the left flank of the 1st Brigade along the spur towards Chivy. The Welch and South Wales Borderers were sent forward, the former on the left, to link up, if possible, with the right wing of the 6th Brigade (2nd Division), which at this time was slowly advancing against serious opposition north of Verneuil. The Gloucesters were held in Brigade Reserve under shelter of the south-west end of the Troyon—Chivy ridge. A large column of Germans were at the time advancing to make a determined assault on the right flank of the 6th Brigade, and the Welch came under heavy machine gun and artillery fire, and suffered considerable casualties. The Gloucesters, being protected by the slopes of the ridge, were luckily not affected. D Company, under Major Gardner, which arrived first, was sent off almost at once to the right flank of the Brigade, to fill up a gap between the South Wales Borderers and the left of the 1st Brigade. For the time this Company was then placed at the disposal of General Maxse, commanding the 1st Brigade, and was retained by him as a brigade reserve. The Battalion had not all come up when a German counter attack threatened the left of the recently occupied position. A and B Companies were ordered forward, with the support company of the Welch Regiment, to repulse the attack. This was, however, beaten back by the front line troops, ably supported by the gunners.

At noon the 1st Brigade was once more heavily engaged, and B Company was moved off to the right, and together with C Company, all under Major Ingram, reinforced the weak spot. They got into a quarry, from which three platoons were pushed forward to fill a gap. Fire was opened on the enemy retiring from the woods up the opposite slope. There was no further hostile infantry movement and the advanced platoons were able to be withdrawn into the quarry, not, however, before several casualties had been inflicted by shell fire during the movements.

At about 4 o'clock in the afternoon, Sir Douglas Haig ordered a general advance, and from then until dusk there was continuous and most confused fighting, which eventually ended in a decided success for the I Corps. At 6 p.m. the situation allowed of the three detached companies of the Gloucesters to be withdrawn, and to rejoin the Battalion. At this period there seems to have been some misunderstanding as to the position of Battalion Headquarters. A Company had been moved back to Vendresse, where it was joined by D Company, and together they formed part of the Divisional Reserve. Major Ingram, Captain Radice and a portion of the B.H.Q. staff were at this point. B and C Companies, on their return from the right flank, reported to Colonel Lovett, at the original Battalion Headquarters at the end of the Chivy spur where also was the Brigadier and part of his staff. (Captain Jenkinson, the Brigade Major, had been killed earlier in the day.)

At dusk the Welch and South Wales Borderers were able to make another slight advance, which brought them to a position just short of the Chemin des Dames. The Welch succeeded in taking many prisoners and two machine guns.

B and C Companies of the Regiment, led by the Brigadier himself, then advanced round to the west of the Chivy spur and up through Chivy village. One platoon of the Welch Regiment also accompanied the column, having been detailed as escort to General Landon. On arrival at a point very near the Chemin des Dames, a post of the enemy was suddenly spotted about 50 yards away. Captain Temple, commanding C Company, pulled the General off his horse, and shouted to his Company behind to clear the road and line the ditches on either side. A shot was fired by someone on the right front, and then followed a general burst of fire more or less " into the blue " on either side. When this had died down, it was found the Brigadier was missing, and it was not until some little time later that he was able to creep in from the front, where he had been caught between the two fires. He was then only accompanied by his groom, Private Wichard, of the Gloucesters, the other orderlies and brigade runners being missing. After this short and unexpected encounter, B and C Companies withdrew slightly to the cover of the woods, and entrenched themselves at the head of the Chivy valley to the right of the South Wales Borderers. Here a line of trenches was dug—the general line of the enemy having been pointed out by an officer of the Black Watch. Just before dawn it was discovered these were facing the wrong way, and there was only just time to withdraw further to the edge of the wood and hastily throw up another line. This position luckily proved suitable, whereas others dug by the South Wales Borderers were found to be useless in the daylight, and had to be vacated. B Company sent out two platoons in observation, one on each flank of the South Wales Borderers. A and D Companies remained throughout the night in reserve at Vendresse.

<small>14th Sept.</small>

On the 15th September the left wing of the British Army again attempted to advance to a point in line with the I Corps, but again were unsuccessful. This had the effect of encouraging the enemy to try and drive back the I Corps, and accordingly most of this day was spent by the 1st and 2nd Divisions in beating off a series of counter attacks.

The Germans made several efforts to break through the line of the 3rd Brigade, and the front was heavily shelled at periods with " Black Marias " or " coal boxes " from the heavy guns newly arrived from the siege of Maubeuge. One shell landed very near to General Lomax. He was entreated by his staff to go either back or further forwards, but remained in the vicinity, and in touch with the situation. Chivy, where were Brigade and Battalion Headquarters, was heavily shelled with shrapnel at intervals.

At dawn B Company was sent forward to a slight spur to fill the space between the Welch and the South Wales Borderers. From their position they were able to carry out some very successful sniping.

At about 10 a.m. there were signs of a German attack. The enemy appeared to be massing just behind the skyline, and some odd detachments advanced. At one time part of the Welch were slightly driven back, and a company of the South Wales Borderers was sent forward between them and B Company to assist. At midday, or soon after, the situation became normal, and with the exception of a few posts left out on the ridge for observation, B Company was withdrawn to the cover of a quarry. In the evening, however, they returned, and were ordered to dig in on the crest.

Lieutenant Swanick was killed during the day by shell fire. Lieutenant Somerset was wounded in the head, and Lieutenant Duncan very slightly hit in the arm; the latter officer was able to remain at duty. Amongst the rank and file there were also a number of casualties during the two days' fighting. One N.C.O. was killed and 15 wounded; 9 other ranks killed, 57 wounded and 2 missing, making a total of 84. The Colonel's charger was also killed on the 15th.

The following two messages were received by units of the 1st Division on the second day of the struggle. " The Major-General received last night the commendation of Sir Douglas Haig on the operations of the 1st Division yesterday. The credit of this lies with the troops, for, in spite of very severe losses, they maintained the very important position which they had occupied, and nobly upheld the best traditions of the British Army." " The following message received by I Corps from Field-Marshal Sir J. French, begins : ' I wish to express my warmest appreciations of the conduct of the 1st Army Corps under General Sir D. Haig throughout the last two days' battle on the Aisne. It is owing to their intrepid advance and splendid resistance to all counter attacks, that we are now able to secure the passages of the river. I heartily congratulate Generals Lomax and Munro and their gallant Divisions upon their splendid behaviour.' "

On September 16th there was somewhat of a lull on the British front, and as the 6th Division had now arrived, and was available as a reinforcement, Sir John French contemplated a further attack on the Chemin des Dames with the idea of relieving the pressure on the II and III Corps. As, however, the Fifth French Army were forced to

16th Sept. fall back somewhat on the right of the 1st Division, and had exposed that flank, the idea of a fresh offensive had to be postponed for the time. The weather was gradually becoming worse and worse; rain was falling most days, and did so solidly from the afternoon of the 15th until the evening of the 16th. The roads and trenches were under water, and the whole country was gradually becoming a quagmire. The nights also were getting exceedingly cold, and the men still had had no fresh issue of greatcoats.

At dawn A Company relieved B Company in the front line, but the latter company remained in support under the bluff behind the trenches, and dug-in in a deep ravine, while C Company made trenches for itself alongside the road.

During the afternoon the Welch came in for a heavy bombardment, and their trenches unfortunately were so sited as to provide very little cover from this particular fire. A new enemy battery seemed to have arrived in the vicinity of Courtecon, and from 6 a.m. had inflicted a number of casualties along the 3rd Brigade front. At 5 p.m. there was a general retaliating shelling by the British guns, which lasted for about half an hour.

From this period onwards the digging of deep trenches became essential as a protection against the enemy's artillery. The lack of the necessary tools was greatly felt in the early days, especially as so many of the small issue from mobilisation stores had already been lost, and the supply not as yet made good. Luckily, the chalk of the Aisne district was comparatively easy to excavate, and, as has been mentioned, the number of caves and quarries were used to the greatest extent possible.

The casualties in the Battalion on the 16th were all in A Company, and amounted to 12 (6 killed and 6 wounded). One light draft animal belonging to the S.A.A. cart was severely wounded, and broke loose.

Second-Lieutenant Baxter and Sergeant Durham, of A Company, both did good work during the day. The latter was conspicuous in the manner he handled his platoon when they came under a heavy enfilade artillery fire. Sergeant Rickards (A Company) did well when in command of an observation post. He continued to send back valuable information, even when the enemy were making an attack on his Company's trenches. Another man to be noted on the 16th was Drummer Fluck, who carried messages backwards and forwards under heavy shell fire in a most gallant manner. He was mentioned in Sir John French's first despatch.

September 17th started peacefully, except for the usual German shelling. This continued unabated all day. During the morning C Company came in for an hour's bombardment, but sustained no casualties. B Company once more relieved A Company, and occupied the front trench line. In the afternoon firing was heard further to the east. The enemy had launched another attack with three battalions, to try once more to oust the right flank of the 1st Division. The brunt of the attack fell on the Northamptons, of the 2nd Brigade, and the 1st Queens, to their right, who were attached to the 2nd Brigade for the time being. These two battalions, aided by the King's Royal Rifles, counter-attacked, and drove the enemy back up the hill. More of the enemy were discovered in line at the top, but their position was enfiladed by the Queens, and they fell back with heavy losses. At 4.30 p.m. the Gloucesters were ordered to move in support of the 2nd Brigade. B Company having been relieved by the South Wales Borderers, the Battalion assembled in Chivy village, and moved off at about 7.15 p.m. towards Troyon. The 2nd Brigade area was reached after an hour's march, and two companies, C and D, were put in position straight away along the Chemin des Dames, to fill a gap between the Northamptons on the right and the Queens on the left. The other two companies remained in support some 200 yards in rear, sheltered under some banks. Later, B Company was detailed to fill in some German trenches which were a short distance in front of those occupied by D Company. After two attempts they succeeded in filling up most, and at the same time buried many German dead and three abandoned machine guns. One gun and a German drum were brought back. Lieutenant B. F. R. Davis, who was in command of the covering party, was wounded in the arm during this operation. The firing at his party alarmed the companies in the main line, and they also opened fire. A Company were even called up to help repulse the expected attack. Sir John French, in his despatch describing the battle of the Aisne, specially mentioned this advance, and the filling in of the trenches.

17th Sept.

The only other casualties suffered on the 17th was a slight wound to Captain Rising, and two men wounded in A Company.

September 18th may be considered the last day of the actual Battle of the Aisne. During this day the Germans delivered several heavy attacks against the I Corps, but it was realised that frontal attacks with opponents so evenly numbered could not succeed, and that while other and more promising objectives should be sought out away on the western flank of the Allies, the great thing on the Aisne was to dig and dig, and get under cover.

The enemy shelling continued most of the day, and though the Queens suffered somewhat heavily, the fire against the Gloucesters was ineffective. In the evening, at about 10 p.m., Major Gardner reported that the enemy were advancing. The Battalion stood to arms, and two companies of the King's Royal Rifles were moved up in reserve. The attack, however, failed to materialise, though further to the east a half-hearted one was carried out on the left of the 2nd Brigade. At about 11 o'clock the Coldstream Guards came up and relieved the Queens from the trenches to the left of the Battalion.

One lance-corporal and two men of C Company, and one man of A Company, were wounded during the day.

On the following day, the 19th, the German shelling was even more severe, and the Coldstreams were badly knocked about. One man of C Company was wounded at the same time.

In order to bring the 1st Division up to strength again after the heavy fighting of the last week, the Commander-in-Chief decided to send up the 18th Brigade from the newly-arrived 6th Division. They arrived in the evening, and commenced to take over the trenches of the 2nd Brigade. At about 7.30 p.m. two Companies of the 2nd D.C.L.I. relieved C and D Companies of the Gloucesters, and the whole of the Battalion moved back to the 3rd Brigade area, north of Chivy, and ceased to be attached to the 2nd Brigade. At Chivy they relieved the Sherwood Foresters (also of the 18th Brigade) in the quarries on the ridge to the west of Troyon.

Before leaving the sector on the right, Privates Orr and Law, of D Company, both distinguished themselves by going out and bringing back a wounded scout. They had to cross a hundred yards of open ground swept by shell fire. They both received the D.C.M., and were, accordingly, the first men of the Battalion to receive awards in the War.

On 20th September the usual German shelling began at 6 a.m., and continued throughout the day. It was soon very evident that ample artillery was necessary in this new type of fighting, which much more resembled siege-warfare than anything the British Army had been engaged in since the days of Sevastopol. A few days later four batteries of 6in. heavy howitzers did arrive from England, and assisted, as far as possible, in countering the enemy's artillery superiority.

The right of the 18th Brigade was temporarily driven back owing to the retirement of some French Algerian troops on their immediate right. However, with the help of the 4th Cavalry Brigade, the line was restored in the afternoon. In front of the Battalion the Germans were quiet, and at night, patrols sent out came back to say that there was no sign of the enemy, but that an eastward movement of transport could be heard.

After dark, Lieutenant C. D'A. S. Bush, 3rd Battalion, joined, with 96 other ranks. He was posted to B Company, and the men distributed throughout the Companies to complete the casualties as far as possible. The losses during the day amounted to 1 man killed and 5 wounded.

Early in the morning of the next day the South Wales Borderers were withdrawn from their position at the head of the Chivy valley, and were brought in on the left of the

20th Sept. Gloucesters. D Company was relieved by a portion of them, and was brought back in support behind A Company. The situation during the day remained unaltered, though further to the east an attack was delivered on the right of the 18th Brigade. The line was, however, immediately retaken.

At about 3 p.m. the East Yorkshire Regiment, on the right of the Battalion, advanced to deliver a counter attack, but was driven back, with some loss by shell fire.

Lieutenant Caunter and 10 men rejoined on the 21st from the rest camp at Le Mans, having been discharged from hospital.

During the night patrols were constantly sent out, but no movement of the enemy could be discovered.

The next few days passed uneventfully, most of the German energy being expended against the Sixth French Army to the west of Soissons.

Patrols were sent out whenever possible to gain information, or to snipe at and worry the enemy. The following officers, N.C.O.'s and men were specially noted for their good work in some daring and useful reconnaissances:—Lieutenant Wetherall, 2/Lieutenant Watkins, Sergeant Tansill, Corporal Elliott, and Private Baker, of C Company; and Lieutenant Young, Lance-Corporal Crabb, and Privates Orr and Bagwell, of D Company. A number of these were mentioned in despatches in the near future.

Second-Lieutenant D. A. Greenslade, 3rd Battalion, joined on the 24th, and was posted to A Company.

On the 25th the arrival of some thousands of German reinforcements from Brussels and Verdun somewhat revived the hostile activity along the Chemin des Dames, and on the 26th and for the following few days the 1st Division was heavily bombarded and attacked.

At about 4 a.m. on the 26th the 2nd Brigade, who had once more taken over the extreme right trenches of the Division, were attacked. At the same time the Queens opened fire on a few Germans on their front. Half an hour later B Company reported that about 40 Germans were moving west across their front, and soon after C Company sent back to say that about 200 of the enemy were massing in front of the Queens, and were entrenching in front of the 2nd Brigade, further to the east. At 7 a.m. A Company observed a line of Germans taking up an extended position in front of the Battalion, and reported that two hostile machine guns had fired a few rounds at them from their left front. Information had previously been received that an attack seemed to be developing against the left of the South Wales Borderers, and it appeared that this was to be general against the front of the 3rd Brigade. Two platoons of D Company, and two companies of the East Yorks were sent off to support the South Wales Borderers, who received the brunt of the storm. At about 9.30 D Company reported over 200 of the enemy were collecting at the head of the Chivy valley, opposite to the Queens. This regiment was immediately informed, but fire was withheld by the Gloucesters, as it was seen that a sudden opening of fire from the Queens at the exact moment would be far more effective. The column was allowed to come to within 50 yards, and was then absolutely mown down by rapid fire. The few who did escape were mostly dropped by fire from the Gloucesters. Although a solid mass of grey could be seen by all the men in the Battalion's trenches, so well disciplined were they that not a shot was fired before the order was given. The machine gun section and the supporting artillery also brought fire to bear on the locality. At much about the same time the German shelling became heavier and heavier, and extended to include the trenches of the Battalion. This continued until about 5 p.m. The first shell burst just in front of the trenches, where a group of officers happened to be standing. Lieutenant Morley, R.E., who had come up to arrange about obstacles, was killed, and 2/Lieutenant Watkins was slightly wounded in the shoulder. Major Gardner, Captain Rising, and Lieutenants Caunter and Duncan were all knocked down by the explosion. About 7 men of C Company were also hit. The total casualties during the day amounted to 27.

No actual attack was in the end delivered against the front of the **26th Sept.** Gloucesters. The only two attacks in the vicinity were those against the South Wales Borderers and the Queens. The former battalion suffered fairly heavy casualties, but in both cases the enemy were repulsed with much heavier losses, and were caught each time by the artillery of the 2nd Division.

During the night patrols were again frequently sent out, but all remained quiet. A patrol of C Company discovered that the Germans had been sapping forwards, and had begun to construct a trench about 200 yards in front of the Queens, but just behind the skyline. They had been shelled out of this position, leaving some 30 dead. Nowhere had they been able to dig down more than about 18 inches.

At about 1.30 p.m. on the next day the Queens reported a large number of the enemy were occupying a trench about 200 yards to their front, presumably this half-dug one. The line was immediately shelled, and the Germans once more forced to withdraw. In front of C Company the ground appeared free from the enemy.

During the afternoon of the 27th orders were received to the effect that the 1st Brigade would relieve the 3rd Brigade during the night, and that battalions would proceed to the following various villages for billeting:—Brigade Headquarters, Queens and South Wales Borderers to Œuilly, Gloucesters to Bourg and the Welch to Courtonne.

At about 11.30 p.m. the Black Watch relieved the Regiment, and companies marched independently down to Bourg, where they took over the billets of the Camerons. The village was actually in the administrative district of the 2nd Division, and the headquarters of that division was also billeted there.

By about 1.30 a.m. on the morning of the 28th three companies had arrived, but before they could settle in, were ordered to stand to arms. Further determined attempts were being made to capture the trenches of the 1st Division, and there was a good deal of rifle and artillery fire heard at the front. However, after a time this died down, the attack having failed, and the whole Battalion was able to get into its billets.

On the 29th September the Battalion got orders to move to Pargnan, a village about two miles further to the east. Accompanied by the cookers and three S.A.A. carts, they marched off by platoons at 500 yards interval, and got through safely without casualties by about 3 p.m. The rest of the transport followed after dark.

Pargnan was the headquarters of the 18th French Colonial Division. Several of their tirailleurs were billeted in the place, and were continually bartering bread for cheese and biscuits with their British comrades. Two heavy guns and batteries of 75's were also in position on the ridge above the village.

On the following day the Welch were also moved into billets in Pargnan, and the whole Brigade was accordingly closed up in the district of Œuilly—Pargnan.

On the 1st October the Battalion was at last re-equipped with greatcoats and packs. When these were first discarded, seven weeks before, on August 25th, the weather was oppressively hot, and even by night the coats were not missed. By the end of September, after days and days of rain, and nights of cold, the lack of them caused much suffering amongst the troops, and must have been responsible for a certain amount of the sickness which occurred.

After church parade on this day the Commanding Officer was sent for by the Division, and at about 5 p.m. orders were given out for the Battalion to move to Moulins, to be in Divisional Reserve. They marched off with the transport in rear, and on arrival at Moulins, A and D Companies and the machine gun section were at once pushed forward to the head of the valley, north of the village, to fill a gap between the right of the 2nd Infantry Brigade, who were entrenched on the Chemin des Dames, and the left of the French line. By night this position was held by two platoons up in front, and the remainder of the companies in close support behind. By day, however, only an observation post was required in the front trenches. The rest of the Battalion found billets in Moulins itself, and here they stayed for several days, with no changes.

4th Oct.

On 4th Oct., B and C Companies were relieved. Lieuts. T. R. A. Morris and J. F. L. Hartmann, both from the 3rd Batt., joined this day, and, being posted to B and C Companies respectively, went up to join their men in the Moulins valley.

During the next three nights one company was detailed to complete some trenches on the spur to the north-west of the village. The task had to be done at night, to avoid observation by enemy aircraft. The machine gun emplacement constructed on this spur was damaged by shell fire on the 8th, and had to be repaired by a platoon of B Company during the evening. Companies not in the front position were made as comfortable as possible in their billets, and blankets were issued.

On October 6th commissions were granted to the following W.O.'s and N.C.O.'s of the Battalion for their capability and continual good work. C.S.M. Hodges, Corporals Brown, Forbes, and Stevens; the first two were gazetted to the Gloucesters.

On October 8th, Captain Radice's appointment as Adjutant came to an end. He was, however, appointed Acting-Adjutant until his successor, Lieutenant J. H. Scott-Tucker, arrived from England. This is an opportunity to mention once more the unceasing energy with which Captain Radice performed his most arduous duties as Adjutant. Not only were his tasks by day continuous and heavy, but it was almost the invariable rule during the Retreat from Mons that orders for the following day never reached units until about midnight. The result was the issuing of orders to companies and transport, etc., whilst the rest of the Battalion was probably enjoying its well-earned rest. The Regiment has much to thank Captain Radice for in those days, as was realised by Colonel Lovett when he forwarded his name for recommendation earlier in the month.

Besides the persons already mentioned as having done good work, the following names were also submitted at this period for displaying particular energy or bravery at one time or another :—Major Ingram, Captain Temple ; Corporal Ryder, Privates Sexton, Pardoe and Parkes (B Company), Sergeant Smith (D Company).

Early in October, Sir John French began to press for the British Army to be positioned once more on the extreme left of the Allied line. In this position it would be nearer to the coast and its Base ; also, its lines of communication would not cross those of the French armies. Further British divisions were expected in the near future, and if the original three corps remained sandwiched between the French troops on the Aisne, and new divisions were sent elsewhere, it would result in a divided command, and many difficulties. General Joffre fully agreed, and from about the 3rd October the B.E.F. was gradually able to carry out its move to the northern wing of the Franco-British battle line.

The Cavalry, the II and the III Corps, were the first to leave the Aisne, and it was not until the 14th that the relief of the I Corps could be commenced. On this day it was reported that the 38th French Division would take over the trenches of the 1st Division. Up to this date the situation north of the river had remained unaltered, and the trench system had become an excellent example of what was to continue throughout the warfare of the next three years. The French on the right of the Gloucesters' position had been driven back slightly on the 10th, but had advanced the line again on the 12th, and subsequent days, so that once more it continued the line of the Battalion along the Chemin des Dames. The Gloucesters' own position had, however, remained throughout unchanged, and they continued to face north-east to protect the right rear of the British Army. This duty, actually, was performed by each half of the Battalion for tours of three days.

At about 10 a.m. on the 15th a French brigadier and the major commanding one of the battalions of the 53rd Regiment came up to reconnoitre the position, and orders were received for the relief to take place that night. Most of the 1st line transport was sent off to join the Train, and at 6 p.m. B and C Companies, who were not in the line at the time, were sent out under Captain Temple to occupy the alternate trenches astride the Moulins—Vendresse spur, to cover the relief. By about midnight the French had

taken over the line of the 2nd Brigade, and had connected up with the Zouaves 16th Oct.
on their right on the Paissy ridge. Unfortunately, the enemy tumbled to what
was happening, and shelled the back areas heavily. Several bodies of French were caught
in fours, and terribly knocked about. About a hundred had been slaughtered to the
left rear of the Gloucesters. In spite of the resulting delay, A and D Companies were
able to fall back by platoons to a point immediately south of Moulins. B and C Companies
then got the order to close in, and by 3 a.m. the Battalion was ready to move off. A
quarter of an hour later they marched south over the Aisne at Bourg, and *via* Dhuizel
to Paars. Here the Regiment halted, and billeted in two farms south of the village.
Here, also, the following message was received from Sir Douglas Haig :—

"I wish to congratulate the 1st Division on the work done while on the Aisne."

On the 17th the Battalion paraded at 4 a.m., and marched *via* Bazoches and
Loupeignes to Fere-en-Tardenois, where they entrained. The train left at 2.13 p.m.,
and passing through Paris, Amiens, Abbeville, and St. Pol, arrived at Cassel at 3.30 p.m.
on the 18th. Here the Battalion detrained, and marched off north-east to the small
village of Longue Croix, where billets were found.

On the following day a draft of 51 men joined the Battalion from England under
Lieutenant J. H. Scott-Tucker and 2/Lieutenant H. K. Foster. Lieutenant Scott-Tucker
took over the Adjutancy, and enabled Captain Radice to take over the command of
B Company. Lieutenant Foster was posted to C Company.

The Battalion on this day, the 19th October, numbered 26 officers and about 1,000
other ranks.

The remainder of the I Army Corps had also begun to arrive about St. Omer and
Hazebrouck, and by the 19th the concentration was completed, the 1st Division being
about St. Omer and Cassel, whilst the 2nd Division lay between Poperinghe and
Steenvoorde.

The 7th Division during these days had been hard pressed, especially about Zonnebeke, north-east of Ypres, where they joined up with the French cavalry under de Mitry.
The wisdom of Sir John French's decision to push the I Army Corps north towards
Ostend and Bruges, instead of actually strengthening the immediate left of the II Army
Corps south of Ypres, became very apparent on the 21st October, when the 22nd Brigade
of the 7th Division were forced back to a line west of Zonnebeke by the unexpected
appearance of two fresh German corps.

The 1st Division on that day were ordered to take Poelcappelle, while the 2nd
Division on their right were to make for Passchendaele. The 3rd Brigade, after spending
a night at Poperinghe, were very early on the morning of the 21st ordered north-east.
Passing through Elverdinghe, Boesinghe and Pilkem, the Gloucesters, who were acting
as advanced guard to the Brigade, arrived at the outskirts of Langemarck at about 8 a.m.
Orders for an attack on the enemy about Poelcappelle were then issued, and the advance
was continued in the following order :—The Queens moved north-east astride the Ypres—
Staden railway, with Poelcappelle Station as their objective ; the South Wales Borderers
deployed on their right, and made for the village itself. The Welch were in support,
whilst the Gloucesters, after their advanced guard duties earlier in the morning, were
put in reserve to the Brigade.

The attack progressed slowly but steadily in face of considerable shell fire, which
was difficult to locate on account of the flatness and enclosed nature of the country. A
hostile infantry advance from the north was now observed, and the French cavalry were
gradually being driven in, exposing the left of the 3rd Brigade. As a result of this threat,
the Gloucesters, who had remained south of the Hannebeek, a small stream just short
of Langemarck village, were instructed to send forward a company to act as a left flank
guard. Accordingly, B Company, under Captain Radice, was advanced, and directed
to occupy Langemarck railway station, and to look after this exposed side.

21st Oct. The village itself came in for a more violent shelling with H.E., while a French battery took up position near the station to help forward the advance.

At about 10 a.m. the remainder of the Battalion advanced in support of the Queens. C Company (Captain Temple) pushed through the village and along the road leading north-east through Koekhuit to Staden. D Company (Major Gardner) was on the right of C Company, and advanced between the road and the railway. B Company, as already mentioned, was in position on the left flank, while A Company, under Captain Rising, remained in battalion reserve south of Langemarck.

The advanced guard of C Company, under Lieutenant Wetherall, occupied the hamlet of Koekhuit, on a small rise of ground about 2,000 yards to the north of Langemarck by about 10.30 a.m. There was very little opposition from Koekhuit itself, but a considerable rifle fire from the direction of Mangalaere, further to the west, caused several casualties. D Company, on the right, with No. 13 Platoon, under Lieutenant Young, in advance, were held up at the start by the difficult and enclosed country which they had to cross. Time was lost in closing men up to pass through gates and gardens on the outskirts of the village, and by the time the leading platoon was able to deploy again, there was no sign of C Company on the left. Lieutenant Young, knowing, however, that his task was to keep in touch with C Company on his left, and to link up with the Queens on or about the Staden railway line on his right, pushed ahead under a certain amount of unaimed rifle fire, and eventually caught sight of Lieutenant Wetherall's platoon on the rising ground to the left.

Further away on this flank, Captain Capel had by this time taken up a position with half C Company on the right of the hamlet of Koekhuit. Captain Temple went up to the village soon after to see Lieutenant Wetherall's dispositions, and as a result of the uncertainty of the enemy's strength on the left flank, ordered up his last platoon. About midday the enemy launched his first attack from the direction of Mangalaere. This was stopped by the portion of Lieutenant Wetherall's men who had been placed in a ditch, to face north. The Germans, about 100 in all, attacked by short rushes, but not being able to get within 600 yards, commenced to dig in. They lost some 20 men in the endeavour, and after about half an hour gave up the struggle, and ran back to the hedges and cover about Mangalaere.

The situation at the time of this attack, and during the rest of the day, was much aggravated by a considerable volume of fire coming from the direction of Poelcappelle railway station, which was really intended for the Queens and other troops attacking that locality. Over away on this flank the Queens had been having a pretty poor time of it, and when Lieutenant Young topped a small rise, he was able to see their position away on the right of the railway, some 400 yards off. His platoon stopped there for a short time to fire at the enemy, who, just as that period, had been beaten back by the Queens, aided by rifle fire from C Company up at Koekhuit. Lieutenant Young was seriously wounded at the time, whilst kneeling up to get a better view of the situation. The platoon, however, was led on by Sergeant Davis, and bearing down to the right, pushed on with the remainder of D Company which was just arriving in support.

The situation on this flank was now becoming more serious, and eventually the Queens were forced to retire. As a result of this, the right of D Company had to conform, and a new position was taken up along the line of a ditch facing north-east.

On the left flank, also, things had not been going too well. The French troops on the left of B Company continued to fall back under pressure of the enemy. They were backed up by a party of their cyclists, but reported the woods to their front were full of Germans, who could not be held up. B Company had been pushed further forward, to assist the left of C Company, and A Company, with Battalion Headquarters, advanced through Langemarck to a point about 200 yards north of the level-crossing on the Koekhuit road. The Machine Gun Section, under Lieutenant Duncan, was also sent off to protect the exposed left flank.

About half an hour after the first attack on Koekhuit, Lieutenant Wetherall 21st Oct. received further supports in the arrival of a sergeant and 15 men of the Scots Guards, of the 1st Brigade. These men were posted on the right of the advanced platoons of C Company, and protected their flank, whilst the Queens were falling back.

Captains Temple and Capel were both severely wounded at this time, and the whole situation was becoming serious. At about 2 p.m. a fresh attack was commenced against the village of Koekhuit, this time by some 200 of the enemy coming along the main road from Staden. They were only stopped after considerable difficulty, as by this time Lieutenant Wetherall's defenders were dwindling down in numbers, and the country through which the attack was made was very enclosed, and the field of fire consequently poor. Matters were rapidly becoming worse and worse. Both flanks were threatened by the advancing enemy, and casualties were steadily increasing, partly by sniping fire from the hedges about Mangalaere, and partly by the now continuous fire from the right. Lieutenant Wetherall sent to report this state of affairs to Captain Temple, and learnt for the first time that his Company Commander had been wounded, and was lying in a ditch some 300 yards off. He, therefore, went back to see him, and to ask for reinforcements. C Company were, however, fully occupied, as the other two platoons had already been severely handled when trying to stop the successful German counter attack on the right. Captain Temple was able to explain where Captain Radice, with B Company, was, and suggested that the latter might be able to help. Lieutenant Wetherall consequently went across to Captain Radice, and reported the precarious situation up in Koekhuit. Whilst he was away, the few surviving defenders were seen to be evacuating the place. Captain Radice immediately gave Lieutenant Wetherall about 30 men, and told him to get back and reoccupy the position, which, as long as it could be held, appeared to be the key to the defence. This he succeeded in doing, while B Company occupied Grutesaele Farm, which lay about 250 yards south-west.

By this time it was almost 4 p.m., and the hostile fire on this flank slackened. Machine gun fire was, however, opened on the left of D Company, and soon after, Lieutenant Caunter, who was commanding this portion of the company, spotted through his glasses columns of the enemy about to debouch from a road near the railway, about 700 yards off on the right front. Although the enemy were not actually visible to the naked eye to the men in the trenches, three intense bursts of rapid fire were so well directed, and the fire discipline was so good, that even at this range the attack failed to mature, and no other attempt was made before dusk. In reply, however, the Germans shelled the position, and a few wounded men lying in a ditch were killed. Lieutenant Wetherall, for his stubborn defence and the skill in so disposing his only too scanty men that the utmost was got out of them, was mentioned in Sir John French's next despatch, and was granted one of the first Military Crosses to be awarded in the War.

A./C.S.M. Smith, Sergeant Stevens, and Corporal Burley all ably assisted in repulsing the enemy's attacks on Koekhuit. Sergeant Bray, of B Company, was, also, specially noted for the capable manner in which he led his platoon to support C Company. He maintained his position for several hours under a heavy fire, until ordered to withdraw. His platoon unfortunately suffered 14 casualties.

The line was held until about midnight, when orders were given to evacuate the now pronounced salient, and the Battalion was to withdraw to the farm south-west of Langemarck, where Battalion Headquarters had virtually remained during the day. The withdrawal was carried out with success, though B Company was somewhat delayed owing to the lack of stretcher bearers to bring back the wounded. Before going back, this company captured two young Einjahrige (or volunteers) from a Jager Regiment. These proved to be quite youngsters, with only two weeks' training!

The Battalion was not actually relieved, but the 2nd Welch, who during the day had come off more lightly than the other units of the 3rd Brigade, were constructing a new defensive line just in front of Langemarck. The South Wales Borderers, like the

21st Oct. Queens, had been heavily counter-attacked earlier in the day, and as a result of the fighting, although the originally planned attack on Poelcappelle and Passchendaele had failed, the German advance had been stemmed, and sufficient ground had been gained to enable Langemarck and Zonnebeke to be securely held by the 3rd Brigade and the 2nd Division.

During the day the 1st Guards Brigade had been directed to make good a line facing north from Langemarck as far west as Steenstraate, while the 2nd Brigade were held back in reserve about Boesinghe.

On the whole, the casualties in the Battalion were comparatively light. C Company suffered heavily in officers; out of its original three, only Lieutenant Wetherall remained. Captain Temple died from his wounds the same day, and Captain Capel lost the use of one eye. Lieutenant Young (D Company), who was badly hit in the stomach, was the other officer casualty. The total amongst the other ranks amounted to 48, of which 21 belonged to B Company. C Company had 13 men hit, and D Company 14.

On the evening of the 21st, Captain Radice took over the command of C Company, and the command of B Company devolved on Captain Blunt once more.

October 22nd was a day of comparative rest for the 3rd Brigade. The brunt of the fighting fell further to the left, on the 1st Brigade, where, during the afternoon, the line was broken at Kortekeer Cabaret, at the point where the road from Pilkem crosses the main Langemarck—Bixschoote road. The German attack was a particularly fine feat of arms, being carried out very largely by Einjahrige, of the 46th Reserve Division. These lads, who might almost be compared with our Officers' Training Corps cadets, advanced with the utmost determination, singing patriotic songs, and though suffering appalling casualties, actually succeeded in driving back their seasoned opponents. It was not until the early morning of the 23rd that sufficient reinforcements could be collected to drive them back, and to re-establish the original line.

The Gloucesters spent the 22nd round about the farm just south of the Hannebeek, where they dug in, and constructed part of the Corps Reserve line, which was to be held at all costs. At 9 a.m. one company was ordered to stand in readiness to reinforce the South Wales Borderers south-east of Langemarck. A brigade of 18-pounders took up a position on the right of the Battalion's new line, and unfortunately attracted a certain amount of hostile artillery fire. At about 4 p.m. a large barn, where A and C Companies were billeted, was badly damaged by a direct hit, and 17 casualties were inflicted. Five men were killed, and 12 wounded. Later in the evening one platoon was sent off as escort to the 40th Battery, R.F.A., on the south-west side of Langemarck.

Except for the one disaster, the day passed off quietly in cleaning up, in digging trenches, and in the hundred-and-one odd jobs that crop up after a spell of fighting.

During the night (2.30 a.m.) Captain Rising and two platoons of A Company were sent up to the northern outskirts of Langemarck, in close support of the Welch. The platoons, No. 4 under Lieutenant Hippisley, and No. 3 under Lieutenant Baxter, were used to fill a small gap on the left of the Welch, to link up with the Coldstream Guards, of the 1st Brigade, on the left. The trenches were dug for the most part by A Company, helped by the 26th Field Company, R.E., and stretched on either side of the road, to Koekhuit. No. 4 Platoon was entrenched to the right of the road, while Lieutenant Baxter's occupied the road itself by a shallow trench and a low barricade, and spread out to the left. From this position Koekhuit was in full view for a considerable way, but there was a certain amount of dead ground about 500 yards away, where a small stream, the Kortebeek, flowed across the front between steep banks some five feet high.

For some time the enemy made no attempt to cross the stream, but at 9 a.m., having fired a farm on the south bank, and about 400 yards from the British line, they advanced under cover of the smoke. A party of them at the same time tried to advance down the road itself, led by a man carrying a flag. This man, whoever he was, was soon killed, and the remainder were driven back. It was at about this time that Captain Rising,

seeing how serious the situation was becoming, went back for supports. He **23rd Oct.**
succeeded in diverting Lieutenant Yalland's Platoon, No. 15, which was going
up with the rest of D Company to assist the Welch Regiment further to the right. With
these fresh men he was able to strengthen the line of trenches on the left of the road.

Very soon, however, the situation became even more critical. In front of the Coldstream Guards a ditch leading up from the Kortebeek had not been discovered in the dark by the relieving company. Along this covered approach the Huns had been creeping, and now suddenly took the Guards by surprise on their rear and flank. The Coldstreamers were forced to retire to a fresh position some 200 yards further back, in a turnip field. Here they held on, greatly assisted by the three Gloucester platoons on their right. These platoons, now dangerously exposed on one flank, were attacked again and again. Lieutenant Yalland, of D Company, and Lieutenant Hippisley, of A Company, were both killed, and Lieutenant Baxter dangerously wounded whilst doubling across the road. The casualties amongst the men were almost as severe.

A Company lost 2 N.C.O.'s and 7 men killed, and 2 N.C.O.'s and 22 men wounded, while D Company had 2 N.C.O.'s and 4 men killed, and 3 N.C.O.'s and 9 men wounded. During the day, also, B Company and C Company lost 4 men.

At about 1 p.m. the German attack slackened, and the enemy commenced to retire, covered by his artillery. By 3.30 p.m., but for this shelling, there was no further activity on this sector of the front.

A few days later the Brigadier attempted to get the names of those who had specially distinguished themselves, but so severe had been the fighting, that no one of the original eighty men could be found.

Sergeants Eddy and Knight and Private Crossman, of A Company, and Sergeant Wilson, of D Company, were granted the D.C.M. for gallantry in carrying on the defence of their trenches after all their officers had been shot, and repulsing a very determined attack which reached within 50 yards of them, with great loss to the enemy. The official account which accompanied the award of these honours was almost unique, in that it recorded the gallantry of each member of the two platoons of A Company. The names of Privates Dutton, Robbins, and Taylor, and Drummer Moulder, were also submitted for recommendation for their fine work in reporting the situation under heavy fire, and for collecting and taking up ammunition. Private Parry, also, although wounded in the shoulder, and sent back to Headquarters, returned to the front trenches to conduct an ammunition cart which he had met.

The Brigade Commander, in a letter describing this action in more detail, wrote :—
" We had a great fight yesterday, and were attacked all day—the Brigade did splendidly and inflicted great loss on the enemy. The Queens made a most gallant charge, and the Gloucesters (100 strong) fired over 500 rounds per man, lost all their officers and many N.C.O.'s, had the Germans within 50 yards, and not a man retired. Some of their bayonets were shot off their rifles, and they had over 60 casualties. A grand performance. The Welch also sat out an attack by mobs of Germans, and downed them gallantly."

Lieutenant Baxter was awarded the Military Cross for his share of this gallant little action, and Captain Rising, the Company Commander, was given the D.S.O. for his devotion to duty. But for the manner in which he controlled the defence of his Battalion's trenches, the line must have been penetrated by such a determined attack on the part of the enemy.

One thousand five hundred German dead were counted in front of Langemarck the next day. Including over 600 prisoners, the enemy's total loss could not have been less than 10,000 men during the last three days in this sector alone. Against this figure the British losses in the I Army Corps amounted to about 1,500.

The German official account of the fighting about Langemarck is particularly interesting, as it shows how completely their plans were frustrated. " With the failure of the 46th Reserve Division to gain a decisive victory between Bixschoote and Langemarck

42   THE GLOUCESTERSHIRE REGIMENT

23rd Oct. on the 22nd and 23rd October, the fate of the XXVI and XXVII Reserve Corps was also settled. For the time being any further thought of a break through was out of the question. The troops up to now had met the enemy full of a keen fighting spirit, and had stormed his positions singing 'Deutschland, Deutschland uber alles,' regardless of casualties, and had been one and all ready to die for their country; but they had suffered heavily in the contest against a war-experienced and numerically superior opponent entrenched in strongly defended positions. Even when the last reserves of the Army, the 37th Landwehr Brigade and the 2nd Ersatz Brigade, had been placed at the disposal of the XXVI Reserve Corps, they could only be used to stiffen the defence."

Mention is also made of the "fortress of Langemarck." This in reality was no more than the small trenches hastily constructed by A Company of the Gloucesters and a small party of Sappers.

The remainder of A Company, under Captain McLeod, were sent off at about two o'clock in the afternoon to the left flank to support the Coldstream Guards. By 7 p.m. they reported that they had succeeded in reoccupying the trenches previously lost by the Guards, and were in touch with D Company on their right. During the evening of the 23rd the remnants of the two platoons of D Company, under Captain Burn, and later the Machine Gun Section also, took over the defence of their trenches on the left of the Koekhuit road. Before the relief was possible, many men of D Company were sheltered in the northernmost houses of Langemarck, where Captain Rising's headquarters and the dressing station had been situated. One section was unfortunately knocked out by a direct hit on a cottage on the right of the road. The rest of the Battalion was in the meantime held in reserve in its old position south-west of Langemarck. Lieutenants Yalland and Hippisley, together with many of the men of the Regiment, were buried near the farm used as Battalion Headquarters.

On the 24th, reinforcements from the French Ninth Army Corps started to arrive, and the 1st Division, being relieved by the 87th Territorial Division, was withdrawn to a point south of the Ypres—Menin road, about Zillebeke. The 2nd Division, at the same time moved further south and took over the frontage of the 22nd Brigade of the 7th Division. During the night portions of the 1st Division moved further east, and took over that part of the line originally held by the 7th Division which lay to the north of the Menin road.

This proved to be the final readjustment of the defending force of Ypres during the period covered by the First Battle of Ypres, or, as it is officially called, "Ypres, 1914." The French continued to hold the sector north of the road to Zonnebeke; from here to a point in Polygon Wood, just west of Reutel, lay the 2nd Division. On their right the 1st Division carried on the line south as far as the Menin road, whence the remnants of the 7th Division stretched down to the village of Zandvoorde. From here the line bent back south-east to form the bottom of what was to become the famous Ypres Salient. This last portion was held by the 3rd Cavalry Brigade.

The following order of the day was received from the Commander-in-Chief :—" The Field-Marshal Commander-in-Chief wishes once more to make it known to the troops under his command how deeply he appreciates the bravery and endurance which they have again displayed since their arrival in the northern theatre. In circulation of official information which records the splendid victory of our Russian Allies, he would remind the troops that the enemy must before very long withdraw troops to the East, and relieve the tension on our front. He feels it quite unnecessary to urge officers, N.C.O.'s and men to make determined efforts and drive the enemy over the frontier."

During the day Private Organ, of D Company, was specially recommended for his coolness and speed in carrying messages between Headquarters and his Company. Each time he had to pass through the village of Langemarck under heavy shell fire, and one time, seeing a suspicious person looking through a window of an empty house, he stopped, though the shells were bursting within a few yards of him, and brought the person back to Headquarters. **24th Oct.**

It had been necessary to send up the remainder of D Company to support the Welch on the right of the Koekhuit road. They were, however, relieved by the 74th French Territorial Regiment at about 11 p.m. Lieutenant Caunter's sector could not, however, be reached, owing to very heavy shell fire, which drove back the French troops at the critical moment. He, together with the Machine Gun Section, was able to get away at about 7 o'clock the next morning, and was able to catch up the rest of the Battalion, which was by then marching round from its billets near Pilkem, through St. Jean, to a point on the Menin road about a mile east of the ramparts of Ypres—a point to be known in later years as "Hellfire Corner." Battalion Headquarters were billeted in the White Chateau, and the various Companies in neighbouring farms and buildings. Here, later in the day, the Divisional Commander visited the Battalion, and congratulated them on the fine work of the past three days, and asked if recommendations had been submitted for "mentions." Early next morning, the 25th, a further move east was ordered, and the 3rd Brigade marched in fours along the main road as far as Hooge. The Gloucesters then turned north, and arrived near Bellewaarde Farm about midday. Here the Battalion remained for the rest of the day, and from its position was afforded its first sight of an aeroplane brought down by rifle fire. A 'plane was observed to fly over the lines from the east, and the Guards in front immediately opening fire, succeeded in fetching it down. Unhappily, it turned out to be one of our own naval 'planes, marked not with the usual red, white and blue circles, but with the Union Jack, which was not recognised until too late.

These last two days were not remarkable for any very exceptional fighting. The next day, however, the 26th, the 20th Brigade of the 7th Division, after hours of stubborn fighting south of the Menin road, were driven back from about Kruiseck, and were forced to take up a new position about half a mile nearer Ypres.

At 7.30 p.m. in the evening of this day the Gloucestershire Regiment was moved up to the grounds of Hooge Chateau, and at 10.30 p.m. a further advance was made to the road running north and south through Veldhoek. Here a trench was to be dug in support to the 1st and 4th Brigades. The Battalion remained in this position until the early morning of the 29th, while the transport, under Lieutenant Halford, moved back to Hooge.

The 27th and 28th of October were days of comparative calm—a lull before the storm which was to break out with such violence on the 29th. In spite of this quiet, it had, however, been necessary to send various units of one brigade to assist the weary troops of other brigades or divisions which had been so depleted by the incessant fighting.

The 3rd Brigade (less the Gloucesters) on the 27th relieved for the day the units of the 7th Division between the right of the 1st Brigade and the left of the 6th Cavalry Brigade (between Kruiseck and Zandevoorde). Each unit was instructed to keep as big a local reserve as possible, and a continuous line of trenches was not considered necessary. Every use was to be made of machine guns in the defence of the line. The Queens, who were in reserve, were ordered to send up their guns to assist the Welch. It was not, however, until 6 p.m. on the 28th that the Gloucesters were placed at the disposal of General FitzClarence, of the 1st Brigade.

The Battalion had by this time dug itself in to the north of Veldhoek village, and were in support trenches facing east, and running roughly parallel to, and about 200 yards in front of, the country road leading from the village towards the south-west corner of Polygon Wood.

On the 27th, Lieutenant Hartmann, 3rd Battalion (attached to C Company) was admitted to hospital sick, and five men were wounded—two accidentally, and the others by shell fire. On the following day, Captain A. F. Chapman (transferred from the 2nd Battalion) joined from the base at St. Nazaire, and was posted to C Company. He

28th Oct. brought up with him a draft of 50 men, most of whom were clothed with the old-fashioned black greatcoats, owing to the shortage of khaki ones! The only other incident of the 28th was the witnessing of the capture of a German spy by the Queens. The man was caught in a house in the village of Gheluvelt, just in front of the Gloucesters, but not before he had released a flight of pigeons.

As has already been mentioned, the line east of Ypres ran across the Menin road just to the west of Kruiseck cross-roads, about a mile and a half in front of Gheluvelt. The Menin road formed the boundary between the 1st Brigade on the north, and the 20th Brigade on the south. Working northwards, and slightly north-east from the road, the 1st Brigade was disposed as follows:—The Black Watch, 1st Coldstream Guards, 1st Scots Guards, and the Camerons. On their right the 1st Grenadiers lay immediately to the south of the Menin road, with the Gordons on their right. This regiment linked up in their turn with the 22nd Brigade. In support were the Border Regiment and the 2nd Scots Guards, of the 20th Brigade, distributed on the eastern outskirts of Gheluvelt. The 3rd Brigade, less the Gloucesters, were at the time assembled in Inverness Copse, to the north of the road, and about a mile in rear of Gheluvelt.

At about 8 o'clock in the evening of the 28th, Lieutenant-Colonel Lovett had been ordered to send forward his Machine Gun Section and 60 men to report to the 1st Coldstream Guards of the 1st Brigade at the 9 km. stone near the Kruiseck cross-roads. Lieutenant Wetherall was selected to command this detachment. On arrival at the cross-roads, his men were split up to fill gaps in the line of the Coldstreamers and the Black Watch. Lieutenant Wetherall himself was north of the Menin Road, but his party was extended over a front of some 500 yards, and was on both sides of the road, acting chiefly as a connection between the 1st and 20th Brigades. One of the machine guns was posted about 200 yards north of the road, while the other was practically on the road itself, sited to fire down it.

The following message from Lord Kitchener was forwarded this day to all units :—
" The splendid courage and endurance of our troops in the battle in which you have been engaged during the last five days, and the boldness and capacity with which you have been led, has undoubtedly given the enemy a very severe blow, successfully frustating all their efforts. Let the troops know how much we all appreciate their services, which worthily maintain the best traditions of our Army."

At about midnight of the 28th/29th, orders were received for the operations ordered for the 28th to be resumed on the next day. The 1st Corps was to continue to operate by its left, and the pressure was to begin to make itself felt at 9.30 a.m. Up to that hour active reconnaissances were to be conducted, and preparations made to concentrate artillery fire on the spur running east-north-east from Noord Westhoek.

Soon after this, reliable information was received that the German XXVII Reserve Corps would attack from the direction of Menin at 5.30 a.m. the next morning (29th), and that the " All Highest " himself would be present to urge on his " victorious troops."

At 5.30 almost to the minute the attack commenced. Under cover of a thick fog, which prevented anyone from seeing more than a few yards in any direction, the Huns burst through the line at the point where the Black Watch and the 1st Grenadiers met. The Black Watch were practically annihilated to the north of the road, together with the Coldstreamers and one company of the Scots Guards. The Grenadiers and Gordons, to the south, were in much the same plight. The first definite news the Gloucesters had of the break-through was from Lieutenant Duncan, who came back at about 6.30 a.m. to report the loss of his guns, and to say that the Germans had rushed the Black Watch trenches on the right of the Guards, and had got behind his position. Lieutenant Wetherall and several of his men were wounded during this first attack. At about 7 o'clock, an hour and a half after the storm had broken, a verbal message was received from the 1st Brigade, ordering the Gloucesters to advance due east on to Gheluvelt, and to check the German advance. Lieutenant-Colonel Lovett directed the Companies to

advance, and act more or less independently. It will be remembered that the **29th Oct.** Battalion started from trenches about Veldhoek, and north of the Menin road.
Owing to the fog and the wooded country through which it was necessary to operate, it was extremely hard to keep direction, more especially as the Companies all started forward at slightly different times, and necessarily with no orders other than to retake the trenches in front. As a result of this, also, it will be found that the story of the Gloucesters during this day's fighting is very disconnected, and hard to follow.

C and D Companies were the first to move forward. C Company advanced on the left, and into Gheluvelt Chateau Grounds. Several casualties occurred at the commencement of the move. Captain Radice was hit early on, and in the matter of officers the company was seriously handicapped. Lieutenant Wetherall, as has been mentioned, had already been wounded in the knee. The other two officers of the company, Captain Chapman and Lieutenant Foster, had advanced with a small party to support the Scots Guards on the forward outskirts of Gheluvelt, and had become detached. C Company from now onwards practically ceased to exist as a company, and the few men who had not been hit, attached themselves to other companies, or even to other regiments, so great was the confusion in the mist and stress of battle.

D Company, after its initial advance, eased off to the right, and then pushed along the Menin road. They reached to within 300 yards of the Kruiseck cross-roads, and there helped to rally the shattered remnants of the gallant 1st Brigade. After being heavily shelled, they were attacked again and again from the north-east. Half the company used the main road as a breastwork, and faced north, whilst the remainder made what use they could of a ditch and faced east. The Germans continued to pour men through the gap they had made, and passing some 400 to 500 yards to the north of D Company, seriously threatened their line of retreat. No other British troops were in sight to the north or to the south—just this one small post of gallant men striving to break the flow of the tide. Here we must leave them, and turn to A and B Companies.
A Company, on the left, had advanced close behind C Company to the assistance of the Black Watch and Scots Guards. Little is known of their movements during the early morning. Lieutenant Greenslade, 3rd Battalion, attached to that company, was sent off with a section of his platoon to the left of the Scots Guards. They arrived there all right, and for the time being all was quiet, except for artillery fire. Suddenly, however, at about 10 o'clock, they were attacked from the flank and rear. After an almost useless resistance, all were either killed, wounded or taken prisoner. Captain Chapman and Lieutenant Foster, of C Company, the latter only out of Sandhurst a few weeks, were near by; the former was wounded and captured, and the latter killed. Lieutenant Greenslade, together with Lieutenant Fitzroy, of the Scots Guards, and some 120 men of all units, were also forced to surrender. Amongst them were about four Gloucesters, all slightly wounded.

B Company, during this period, under Captain Blunt, had been far from idle. Advancing close behind D Company, they skirted north of Gheluvelt Church, and leaving the Guards on their left flank, still fighting hard in the Chateau grounds, they crossed the Ypres—Menin road near the windmill at the eastern extremity of the village, and pushed on towards Kruiseck. Fighting most of the way, they succeeded in reaching the rising ground to the south of the road, about 800 yards in front of Gheluvelt. Here they were brought to a standstill, and were slowly driven back by great masses of Huns to a point between the main road and a windmill some 200 yards to its south. During this retirement Lieutenant Harding was fatally hit below the heart. Private Ireland and another man from No. 7 Platoon volunteered to bring in their platoon commander. They succeeded in dressing the injury, but within a few minutes the Germans attacked again. Ireland was wounded in the leg, and his comrade killed by a piece of shrapnel. Ireland, however, bravely stuck to his task, and carried Lieutenant Harding back to safety, only to find the wound fatal.

29th Oct. Turning once more to D Company, whom we left at a point slightly to the north of the furthest east reached by B Company, the same state of affairs existed, and after holding out for so long in the face of the overpowering numbers, Major Gardner was forced to withdraw. Luckily a portion of A Company, under Captain Rising, had been able to advance to a position to the right rear of Major Gardner's Company. These fresh, or rather freshly-arrived, troops were able to cover the retirement of D Company to a second position some 300 yards further back, where another stand was made. Small parties had been cut off—one portion of D Company, under Sergeant Warrick and Corporal Birley (the latter of Lieutenant Wetherall's platoon) had taken up a position to the north of the Menin road. They remained out with seven men, after all the Guards had retired, and were eventually captured fighting to the end.

Soon after noon the remainder of the 3rd Brigade was ordered up to assist the shattered 1st Brigade. The South Wales Borderers advanced on the left, and reached the eastern edge of Gheluvelt Chateau grounds, the Welch pushed through the village itself and occupied the far edge and a portion of the country to the south of the Menin road, while the Queens, who were further south, were able to push ahead, and eventually took up a position to the right front of the Welch. This advance of fresh troops considerably relieved the strain on the Gloucesters, and the Battalion was gradually able to withdraw. A small party of B Company, consisting of Captain Blunt, Lieutenants Morris and Bush, and about twenty-five men, were still out in advance, holding on to a spur, with the windmill some 500 or 600 yards to their right front. They had heard that the 3rd Brigade was to counter-attack, and had gallantly determined to hang on to this advanced post to assist in the attack. Unfortunately the attack failed, chiefly owing to enfilade artillery fire from the direction of Bercelaere, and the Brigade was forced to retire to its original line, about 200 yards in front of the village, where they dug themselves in during the night of the 29th/30th. Captain Blunt's small party was eventually relieved by General Capper in the evening, by the 2nd Queens, of the 7th Division, and withdrew to Veldhoek, where the rest of the Battalion had been concentrated.

Captain Burn, East Surrey Regiment, and attached to D Company since the outbreak of war, was killed during the morning's onslaught. This left only Major Gardner and Lieutenant Caunter to bring the Company back to a position just east of Gheluvelt Church, and later to Veldhoek. A Company had withdrawn much about the same time, and was on the left of D Company.

As may well be realised, the Regiment had become considerably disorganised during the day's continual and confused fighting, but it was fortunate in being directed to assemble soon after 6.30 p.m. at the line at Veldhoek, from which it had advanced twelve hours previously.

The first returns rendered for the casualties for these twelve hours showed 10 men killed, 77 wounded, and 132 missing. Eventually, however, when more accurate figures could be obtained, the total was found to be 167, and was distributed amongst the Companies as follows:—

	Officers.			N.C.O.'s.			Privates.		
	k.	w.	pr.	k.	w.	pr.	k.	w.	pr.
A Company	–	–	1	4	1	2	8	9	7
B ,,	1	–	–	1	4	1	4	15	2
C ,,	1	2	1	3	5	2	16	16	6
D ,,	1	–	–	6	4	3	14	16	11
	3	2	2	14	14	8	42	56	26

Captain McLeod, Second-in-Command of A Company, was now put in command of the survivors of C Company, whilst Lieutenant Duncan, after the loss of his guns, joined his old Company, "A," for duty.

The night of the 29th was luckily quiet, as was the whole of October 30th **30th Oct.** so far as the Gheluvelt sector of the Ypres salient was concerned. There were certainly several alarms, and much Hun aerial activity, but the brunt of the fighting on this day took place further south. The enemy attacked the 3rd Cavalry Division who were holding the village of Zandvoorde, and eventually broke through in this area. The 7th Division, on their left, were also driven back, and a gap was caused. This was filled by two battalions of the 4th Guards Brigade and two from the 2nd Brigade. Several similar moves took place round about the Menin road, to prepare for eventualities.

During the night of 29th/30th the continual rumbling of transport behind the German lines announced the movement of troops, and foreboded no good for the scanty defenders of Ypres. Actually, the XV Corps, followed by the XIII and the II Bavarian Corps, were arriving, to take their share in the battle, which the German Emperor said would be of decisive importance to the War.

On the 30th the two remaining battalions of the 2nd Brigade, the 1st Loyal North Lancs. and the 2nd King's Royal Rifles, were brought up behind Landon's 3rd Brigade, and were held in reserve north and south of the village of Gheluvelt. The Brigade were still situated as on the evening of the 29th—the Welch were responsible for a frontage of about 250 yards immediately in front of the village, with their right resting on the Menin road. On their left were the South Wales Borderers, who linked up with the Scots Guards, and on their right the 1st Queens, who in their turn joined up with their 2nd Battalion of the 7th Division. The Gloucesters still remained in the support trenches about Veldhoek. During the day they lost 7 men killed and 5 wounded (D Company). They had been ordered to hold themselves in readiness to assist the 7th Division, if necessary, and also to continue their line of entrenchment southwards across the Menin road. In the evening they were ordered to be ready to support with the bayonet the Welch or the Queens in case of attack, and to leave no men in support, but to use every one should the enemy succeed in breaking through.

Very early in the morning of the 31st the line was subjected to a very severe bombardment, and at about 6 a.m. the Hun attacks commenced. The church, houses, and windmill of Gheluvelt were reduced to ruins, and the Welch were practically wiped out where they stood, and soon after dazed and broken men of this regiment commenced to straggle back through Gheluvelt and Veldhoek. Whole companies were annihilated, and the marvel was how anyone remained to help break the infantry attacks which were launched again and again.

At about 5.30 a.m. the Gloucesters were ordered to move up one company to join the King's Royal Rifles, who by now had only one reserve company out of the line, the rest having already been absorbed as a support to the Queens. Later, at about 10.30 a.m., the Battalion was ordered to a fresh line slightly further east, and to stretch south to cover the western edge of Gheluvelt village, on either side of the Menin road. Many messages were sent back from units to Brigade Headquarters, asking for reinforcements, but it is very doubtful if many of these ever arrived. As an instance of what was happening behind the lines, the following story of Private Shipway, of the Gloucesters, may well be given. Shipway at this time was one of the battalion signallers attached to Brigade Headquarters, near "Clapham Junction," some 2,000 yards behind Veldhoek. Early in the morning he was given a message to take up to the Regiment from the Brigade Major. An orderly of the South Wales Borderers was also given a note to take to his commanding officer at the same time. They both set out together, but after going a short distance up the Menin road, the South Wales Borderers' orderly was knocked off his bicycle by a bit of shrapnel and killed. Shipway therefore took on both messages, delivered the one to his own unit, and obtained leave to take on the other to the South Wales Borderers, who were up in the front trenches. He had to advance under very heavy shell fire, and along the rear of the trenches for 300 to 400 yards, with little or no cover from fire or view. He safely delivered his message, and obtained a receipt, but

31st Oct. had to wait about two hours before he was allowed to return to his own battalion, owing to the heavy shell fire. He was then wounded in the hand and wrist, but immediately volunteered to take back an answer to the Brigade. For this devotion to duty, and his resource in an emergency, he was awarded the D.C.M.

About midday the Welch and the Queens were driven back further, having been enfiladed by some of the enemy, who had poured through the original gap. The few supporting troops were far too weak in numbers to do any more than to prevent the enemy from issuing from the village, and at the time it was touch and go whether the line could possibly bend any more without completely breaking.

Colonel Lovett was ordered to rally and collect all possible men who were streaming back more dead than alive from the awful shambles up in front. Men from the 3rd Brigade, from the Guards and Black Watch, all mixed up and shaken, were gathered together by Colonel Lovett as they straggled back along the Menin road, and by Major Ingram some yards further back in the woods to the south of the road. Arms were picked up, and as soon as the men had recovered, they were sent forward again. Some Gordons, including a N.C.O. with ammunition mules, came up about this time, and were also directed to their unit south of Gheluvelt. Counter-attacks were organised by the Commanding Officer, and companies acting on their own were able, after desperate fighting, to hold back the Hun; B and D Companies had the hardest of the fighting. The former company, with two platoons on either side of the road, Lieutenant Morris on the north and Lieutenant Bush on the south, were ordered to advance and drive out the enemy from the houses on the western outskirts of Gheluvelt village. This they succeeded in doing, and this portion of the line was held firm until the Battalion was relieved.

D Company, now only 80 strong, was ordered up at about midday and told to recapture a trench which had been lost immediately to the north of the Menin road. The company, under Major Gardner, advanced under a terrific shell fire until they came in sight of the front line trenches. Those immediately in front were safely in British hands, and it was evident that the break had occurred more to the south. Accordingly, Major Gardner led the company across a stretch of extremely open ground to a sunken road, where the few remaining men rallied. There were only 30 left. Knowing the urgency of the situation, Major Gardner decided that he could not wait for the possible arrival of any more men, and so ordered a further advance to the attack. Within a few yards he and 15 men fell, and the remainder under Lieutenant Caunter, were forced to remain in a sunken lane, where they gallantly held out until the Germans swarmed over the position and took prisoners the few who remained alive. It seems highly probable that D Company had somehow pushed forward at a point where there was a gap in the attacking line of Huns. The British front line here had been absolutely wiped out, and the enemy had pushed on. This would account for the fact that no other British troops were visible, and that the Germans who were encountered later were advancing in small columns, and not as attackers in the front line.

During these critical hours Generals French and Haig were anxiously awaiting at Hooge the latest news, and were greatly fearing that the I Army Corps was at last being driven back after the wonderful stand of the last few days. At about 1.30 p.m. a fresh disaster occurred. A shell exploded in the Headquarters of the 1st and 2nd Divisions at Hooge Chateau, killing or wounding the two divisional commanders and six other staff officers. As a result of this, General Landon was called upon to command the 1st Division in place of General Lomax, and in the evening Lieutenant-Colonel Lovett took over command of the 3rd Brigade. Things, then, early this afternoon were looking blacker and blacker, when a Flying Corps officer, after reconnoitring above the Menin road, came back to report in person that the 1st Division line was broken, and that swarms of Huns were pouring through. Even Haig felt that the last had come, and orders were nearly given then and there for the transport to be turned round. This, however, could never be, and orders were actually given to counter-attack.

At 2 p.m. Von Diemling's XV Corps attacked again, and this time the 31st Oct.
right of the South Wales Borderers was wiped out, and the rest of that
battalion forced to retire through Gheluvelt Chateau grounds to the line of the light
railway. They gallantly counter-attacked, and were successful in driving back the enemy
and in taking up a position along the south-east edge of the Chateau woods. At 3 o'clock
the 2nd Worcesters, from the 2nd Division, made a further counter-attack, and, gallantly
led by Major Hankey, cleared the woods north of Gheluvelt, and occupied the northern
outskirts of the village, linking up with the right of the South Wales Borderers.

Great was the astonishment and relief at Hooge when an officer suddenly galloped
up with the news that the 1st Division had rallied, and were again moving forward!
Although the Germans continued to press forward, the line now held firm, and behind
the Gloucesters, at the west end of Gheluvelt, the Queens and Welch were given an
opportunity to rally and re-form. At one time in the early afternoon the enemy suddenly
brought a gun on to the Menin road itself, to fire directly down on to our position about
Veldhoek. Without a moment's delay, Lieutenant Blewitt, of the 39th Brigade, R.F.A.,
galloped one of his guns into position on the road, and opened fire. The Germans got
off one round—our gunners got off two, and the second was a direct hit on the hostile
gun. After this the Gloucesters built a barricade across the road at the Veldhoek cross-
roads, and from this position were busy firing at the masses of Hun troops still advancing
along the road to Ypres.

At about 6 o'clock in the evening orders were given for those troops north of the
road to withdraw to a fresh line stretching from the left of the Gloucesters at Veldhoek,
past Polderhoek Chateau and up to Polygon Wood. The retirement was carried
out without further trouble by 9 p.m., and apparently without the knowledge of the
enemy.

From a doctor who was left behind with the wounded it was learnt afterwards that
the Germans had suffered terribly in the taking of Gheluvelt, and were far too exhausted
and disorganised to push any further during the night.

The casualties on our side were also naturally very heavy, but there is no doubt the
gallant stand of the 1st Division, in which "The Old Braggs'" played such a glorious
and important part, did much to break the fighting spirit of the Huns just at the critical
moment when one extra push on their part would almost certainly have won through to
the Channel ports. The incomparable spirit which was part of the Regiment, and which
prevented straggling and loss of *morale* during the trying days of the 200-mile Retreat
from Mons, still lived in spite of everything.

Of the casualties suffered by the Regiment on the 31st, amongst the officers, B
Company lost Lieutenant Bush wounded, and D Company all its officers—Major Gardner
killed and Lieutenant Caunter missing. Lieutenant Caunter was afterwards reported
as a prisoner of war. In July, 1917, he succeeded in escaping from Schwarmstadt, and
was later awarded the Military Cross for his share in the fighting during this first Battle
of Ypres, and for the manner in which he got clear from the Hun after a thirteen days'
struggle.

Lieutenant Scott-Tucker was wounded during one of the counter-attacks, and as a
result the duties of Adjutant devolved on Lieutenant Halford, the Transport Officer.
The other alteration in Battalion Headquarters on the evening of the 31st was that
Major Ingram assumed command of the Regiment on Colonel Lovett proceeding to take
over the Brigade. The casualties amongst the men amounted to 66, of which nearly half
were suffered by B Company. There were 16 killed, 45 wounded, and 5 taken prisoner.

The next day the following two messages were received from General French, the
first being addressed to the I Corps :—

"I warmly congratulate you and your command on work done yesterday.
Initiative displayed by subordinates cannot be too highly praised, as you justly say.
I deeply deplore your losses."

1st Nov. " The Field-Marshal Commander-in-Chief has watched with the deepest admiration and solicitude the splendid stand made by the soldiers of H.M. the King in their successful effort to maintain the forward position which they have won by their gallantry and steadfastness. He believes that no other army in the world would show such tenacity, especially under the tremendous artillery fire directed against it. Its courage and endurance are beyond all praise. It is an honour to belong to such an army. The Field-Marshal has to make one more call upon the troops. It is certainly only a question of a few days, and it may be only of hours, before, if they stand firm, strong support will come, the enemy will be driven back, and in his retirement will suffer at their hands losses even greater than those which have befallen him under the terrific blows by which, especially during the last few days, he has been repulsed. The Commander-in-Chief feels sure that he does not make this appeal in vain."

November 1st was a day of almost equal pressure in the Salient, but it was chiefly down south at Messines and Wytschaete where the heaviest fighting took place. A portion of the 1st Brigade were temporarily driven from their trenches, and the 3rd Brigade, now complete again with the Gloucesters in the line, came in for a large share of the shelling and infantry attacks.

One of the first sounds of the morning was the crowing of a cock in the village of Gheluvelt, but as this was taken up all along the line, and later joined by cuckoo calls, there is no doubt it was one of the first examples of "animal noises" being used by the Germans in the war as signals. The night of the 31st/1st was also remarkable for the use for the first time of lights other than star shells for illuminating the battlefield. These were soon to devolve into the wonderful firework displays of the enemy and the Verey lights and parachute lights of the British Army.

The barricade across the Menin Road at Veldhoek and the houses on either side provided excellent cover for snipers to pick off the Huns advancing up the road or amongst the ruins of Gheluvelt. Sergt.-Major Long and C.Q.M.S. Mayell did excellent work from one of the houses, and accounted for many of the enemy as they attempted to cross the road from the south. Eventually, however, they were driven downstairs, as the walls were only made of plaster, and several machine-guns had been turned on their position from the right of the road.

There was great eagerness amongst the personnel of Battalion Headquarters, and the transport men, to get a chance of potting the Hun. In many cases this was the first opportunity some of these men had had to use their rifles. A gunner driving up a cart full of small arms ammunition asked to have a shot over the barricade, and, in his excitement, exposing himself too much, got hit himself in the neck.

During the day the signallers did great work from the roofs of the houses, directing the gunners and helping them to down the hostile guns which were sending over for the first time their shrapnel shells which seemed to burst with a double crash.

In the evening the remnants of the 3rd Brigade were relieved by the 2nd Brigade. The Gloucesters handed over their frontage to the K.R.R., and marched back to Inverness Copse, about a mile in rear, and to the north of the Menin Road.

The Battalion was now reduced to between 200 and 300 men. Even on the 1st the casualties had been heavy, and totalled 75 (16 killed, 46 wounded, and 13 prisoners), of which C Company lost the most.

To counteract these losses, Lieutenant Grazebrook rejoined the Battalion during the evening, and brought up a draft of 50 men.

Early on the morning of November 2nd the Brigade fell in, and, about 800 strong, started to march west along the Menin Road to what was expected to be a real rest after the strain and anxieties of the last week. Before the Battalion had even passed through the village of Hooge, about three-quarters of a mile back, a halt was called, and orders issued whereby the whole column wheeled to the south and into Sanctuary Wood. The situation was still too critical to allow of units proceeding out of the immediate vicinity. French troops were certainly arriving to reinforce both the north and south of the Salient, but as yet the 3rd Brigade could not be spared.

2nd Nov.

During the morning considerable firing was heard from the direction of Gheluvelt, but it was not until about one o'clock that orders were given to the Regiment to advance and retake some trenches that had been lost earlier in the morning. The Battalion pushed forwards and crossed to the north of the Menin Road near " Clapham Junction." The enemy were at the time shelling the woods in front with " coal-boxes," or high explosive shells exploding with clouds of black greasy fumes. Rifle fire was spluttering out in the direction of Veldhoek, with the occasional " rat-tat-tat " from a machine gun in a Belgian armoured car travelling up and down the Menin Road just short of the village. No one quite knew the situation up in front, and there was much doubt as to where exactly the enemy had broken through—presumably south of the road, as bodies of cavalry were seen galloping off in that direction, either to fill a gap in the line or to clear the woods of stray Huns.

The next orders were for the Gloucesters to recross to the right of the road, and after slightly reorganising the line under cover of Herenthage Wood, to push north across the Bassevillebeck and up the further slope, in later years called " Tower Hamlets." A Company, under Captain Rising, was left on the north of the road near the pond at Veldhoek Chateau, while B Company slowly advanced through the woods, across the stream, and up the hill to the eastern edge of the undergrowth round the Chateau of Herenthage. C Company, now under Captain McLeod, followed B Company, and coming up on their right, linked up with the few remnants of the Bedfords and Yorks, of the 7th Division. On the left were a small number of French troops, and further away, near the Menin Road, the Black Watch, of the 1st Brigade. Captain McLeod was killed soon after the position was reached, and Captain Blunt, commanding B Company, was also hit in the shoulder, probably by snipers firing from the buildings in front. He was forced to leave the line, but was able to rejoin the Battalion on the evening of the 8th, after spending five days in the C.C.S. at Ypres. Several other casualties occurred about this time through our own gunners not realising that the eastern edge of the woods was now again held by British troops. The trenches, however, in this part of the line were dug very deep and narrow, and had been constructed in two parallel rows with about four yards in between, so that there was very fair cover from shrapnel.

At about 6 p.m., D Company arrived in the valley behind the trenches, now under the direct control of Major Ingram, with Lieutenant Halford to assist him. Major Ingram went forward to try and grasp the situation in front, but there was still considerable doubt as to just where the enemy were, and where exactly the trenches were which had been lost. There was also a tremendous confusion of units—Gloucesters, Welch (who had also come forward under Captain Rees), Bedfords, Yorks, Royal Berks, a scattering of French and Turcos, and nobody in actual command, until General FitzClarence arrived, in the very front line, from the 1st Brigade. His solution was to " push on, find out the enemy, and drive him back." Major Ingram therefore organised the attack, and ordered a general advance against the supposed German position on either side of an isolated building which could be seen some 700 yards away. The first stage of the advance was carried out with success, and it seemed that the whole attack would succeed. Unfortunately, at the further side of the first field to be crossed was a line of trenches, unoccupied except by a few wounded enemy. This line was rushed, and the cheering warned the Germans further back, for when the advance was carried on through the next field there was a sudden burst of rapid fire from the right front, and a line of grey figures could be seen in the moonlight about a hundred yards off in the roots. Firing was then taken up by the enemy in the immediate front, and by the French troops from the rear. These troops had refused to advance without the direct orders from one of their own officers, and were now busy shooting into the backs of the attacking force. The result

2nd Nov. was that the right recoiled, and the whole line fell back to the line of empty trenches. A number of casualties were suffered, and, amongst others, Lieut. Grazebrook was hit by the first burst of fire from the right. Later a second withdrawal was ordered, and the line of double trenches at the edge of the trees was held.

The defence of this line was then reorganised by General FitzClarence, and the 2nd Welch took over the sector held by the Gloucesters, who were brought back into Sanctuary Wood.

The total casualties in the Battalion for 2nd November, in addition to the three officers mentioned, amounted to 58—11 killed, 45 wounded, and 2 taken prisoner.

The night passed off quietly, as did the following day. November 3rd was spent by the Battalion in improving as far as possible the trenches in Sanctuary Wood, and certain of the officers were called upon to go forward to reconnoitre the ground in front of "Stirling Castle" and the western edge of Herenthage Wood, in case it should be necessary to take up a position there in support of the front line troops. During the day a Staff Officer was seen galloping wildly down the Menin Road, shouting out that the Huns had broken through. But it was afterwards suspected that he was a spy, as on that day the enemy made no serious attempt to break through: in fact, the "War Lord" had left, and his efforts to drive the contemptible little army of Britain to the sea had failed.

A and C Companies each had a few casualties through shell fire during the day. In the evening, Captain Pritchett joined the Battalion, bringing with him nearly 200 reinforcements from the Base. These numbers were particularly welcome after the previous week's casualties, and greatly helped to put fresh life into the Regiment, to be called upon two days later to take part in what was to be their final struggle in the Ypres Salient in 1914.

Captain Pritchett was posted to D Company.

Very early in the morning of the 4th November, the Battalion moved up under very heavy shell fire to the support position selected along the near edge of Herenthage Wood, where, under Haig's directions, a series of all-round redoubts had been constructed. The Regiment was not, however, required, and was able to return to Sanctuary Wood later in the morning. The casualties for the day amounted to eleven—2 killed and 9 wounded.

Late at night the Gloucesters relieved the South Wales Borderers in the front line, east of Herenthage Chateau, where they were told they were to hold on for 24 hours at all costs, after which they would be relieved. Except for extremely heavy shelling at different periods of the day, November 5th passed off without further troubles. Supports had been at hand in the morning to reinforce the Battalion frontage, but as there were no signs of an immediate infantry attack, Major Ingram considered the Regiment could well carry on until the evening, when the 3rd Brigade were to be relieved by the 6th Cavalry Brigade. The 3rd Dragoon Guards actually took over the front trenches from the Gloucesters. The losses to the Battalion during the day were exceptionally heavy, considering that they were all caused by artillery fire. Many of the trenches had, however, been completely destroyed, and several men had been buried. The total amounted to 41—13 killed and 28 wounded, of whom D Company lost the most.

The night of November 5/6th was spent in Railway Wood, on the Roulers railway, near Bellewaarde Farm. The next morning was spent in reorganising the Battalion once more. This was only just done in time, as orders were received for a sudden move south towards Klein Zillebeke. Down at this southern end of the Salient the Germans had renewed the offensive. At about 2 p.m., after an unusually heavy bombardment, the 39th Division of the XV German Corps forced back the French troops who were now defending the line to the south of the Zillebeke—Zandevoorde road. As a result of this, the right flank of the Irish Guards, of the 4th Brigade, was exposed. After a gallant defence the Guards were driven in, and a dangerous gap had been formed. An urgent message, however, brought up General Kavannagh's 7th Cavalry Brigade at a gallop from behind Zillebeke. These troops, consisting of the three regiments of the Household Cavalry, threw themselves into the gap, and restoring the position, drove the Huns back for several hundred yards. At this moment the French unfortunately again gave way, and another gap was left on the right, through which the enemy immediately pressed. The Blues, who up to now remained in support, were sent off to this flank, and although a certain amount of the ground regained had to be abandoned, the gap was filled, and Zwartelan and "Hill 60" reoccupied.

6th Nov.

Reinforcements, such as were available, were rushed up to the point of immediate danger. The 22nd Brigade was recalled in motor 'buses from Dickebusch, where it had been held in Corps Reserve. The 2nd King's Royal Rifles, of the 2nd Brigade, were also hurried up, and ordered to relieve a squadron of the Life Guards that was holding the railway line to Armentieres, on the right flank. The Gloucesters left the neighbourhood of Bellewaarde Farm at 4 p.m., and marching *via* Zillebeke, arrived in the dark, and were immediately told to take over from the cavalry north of Zwartelen. The whole movement was very hurried, and no definite orders were given. Direct touch with the remnants of the Irish Guards could not be obtained, though it was known that they were in the woods to the north-west of the village. For some unknown reason the regiment to the south of Zwartelen were at this moment subject to one of those panics which occasionally arise in all warfare when troops are highly strung, and almost at the end of their endurance. In this case, at this very critical moment, a portion of the battalion, whilst advancing on the right of the Gloucesters, suddenly failed, hesitated, and turned. Although its right flank was thus exposed, the Gloucesters were able to push south-east and to occupy the eastern edge of the village and the woods to the north. Lieutenant Halford, with about 60 men—company and platoon organisation had almost ceased to exist,—established a post near a house about 300 yards in advance of the village, and could probably have gone further still. When he had reported his position to Brigade Headquarters, it was, however, decided that the post was too isolated, and had to be withdrawn. The whole situation was most confused, and while it was still dark, although the moon had risen soon after the Battalion had relieved the Horse Guards, the only thing to be done was to consolidate the eastern end of Zwartelen and the woods further to the north. Snipers were posted in the houses, and touch was eventually obtained with the Munsters, in the woods on the left. Major Ingram and the Brigade Major of the 3rd Brigade had discovered their right flank when reconnoitring in this direction. The actual frontage occupied by the Battalion was very large, and could only be divided up roughly into sectors to be held by batches of men, with one of the few surviving officers here and there.

The morning of the 7th was, as usual, very misty, and what little reconnaissance had been carried out in front, proved faulty.

About 6 o'clock orders were received from General Cavan (commanding the 4th Brigade) for the Gloucesters to assist an attack to be made by the 22nd Brigade on the right, by firing into the wood on their left and left front. The order to attack had to be cancelled on account of the fog, as it was absolutely impossible to see more than a few yards ahead. Later on it was reported that the 22nd Brigade had captured their objective, and it was stated the trenches opposite the Gloucesters were empty. The Battalion accordingly pushed forward in two lines, Captain Rising leading the first, and Major Ingram the second, about 50 yards behind. The rest of the 3rd Brigade were to support this advance. On issuing out of the village of Zwartelen, the Battalion was met by an intense rifle and machine gun fire, and it was found that the enemy were holding some of the eastern detached houses of the village.

The whole advance had been too hurried, and no definite orders had ever been given. Officers and men were much too exhausted to do more than to clear a few of the houses. Most of the men had to lie down in the open all day, and only a few could get back to

7th Nov. the trenches they had dug the night before. Major Ingram and Lieut. Halford tried to check the tendency to retire to the cover of the houses, but there were not enough officers to direct the men forward. Lieut. Kershaw, with his platoon of A Company on the right, had been cut off, and nothing more was ever heard of him. Major Ingram was wounded in the knee whilst crossing the road under full view for the fifth time when attempting to point out the line which was to be held. He was, however, able to crawl to Captain Rising, and discuss with him the situation, before being taken back to the dressing station. Captain Rising himself was carried back to the dressing station a few minutes later, mortally wounded. Later still, Lieutenant Halford was also hit, and the only surviving officers were Captain Pritchett (now commanding), Lieutenant Duncan (acting Adjutant), Lieutenant Morris (B Company), and the Quarter-Master. The number of men who answered their names at roll call that evening totalled 213 (A Company 61, B Company 44, C Company 49, D Company 59). No accurate casualty lists were ever kept or rendered for the fighting of the night of the 6th or for the 7th of November, but it is estimated that 43 men were killed, 47 wounded, and 8 taken prisoners. A Company was the one to suffer the most.

Amongst the many who distinguished themselves during these days at Zillebeke, Lance-Corporal Royal was specially noted. On the outbreak of the War he was a bandsman, who, with the other members of the band, became one of that small group of gallant men who acted as stretcher bearers and tended to the wounded. On 7th November Lance-Corporal Royal had organised a first aid post in a cottage behind Zwartelen, and throughout the day had carried out his task under very heavy shell fire. When shells fell on the roof of the building, he supervised the removal of the wounded to a position of greater safety with the utmost coolness and courage. During the day the stretcher bearers of the Gloucestershire Regiment collected the wounded not only of their own battalion, but also of the Welch and of a French regiment. From all these men Lance-Corporal Royal was selected for his gallantry and ability, and was awarded the D.C.M.

Major Ingram's name should also be brought forward at this time, although it was not until 1916 that he received his D.S.O., and was mentioned in Despatches for his services during the First Battle of Ypres. He had taken over command of the Battalion from Colonel Lovett on October 31st, and for the last week had been largely responsible for the manner in which the Gloucesters had held their own in defence, and had driven back the Hun whenever humanly possible. It was a misfortune that there was no senior officer on the spot to note the manner in which he led his men, and the example he set, and to recommend earlier the awards which he so gallantly won during those days of 1914.

Captain Bosanquet joined the Battalion with 20 other ranks during the night of the 7th, and so brought up the total of officers to four. He immediately took over the duties of Adjutant, and held this post until he was wounded in December. It was when he was wounded this time that the War Diary for November was looted out of his valise, and, as a result, much valuable information lost.

On Sunday, November 8th, having been relieved by the cavalry, the remnants of the Gloucesters marched back to Herenthage Wood, where they remained for two days in close support of the 1st Brigade.

Captain Blunt rejoined the Battalion during this period, but no fresh men arrived to fill up the gaps in the ranks. There had been, unfortunately, no drafts sent out from England for the Regiment since October 3rd, and the next, of 200 men, was not to embark until 11th November. However, the rest from actual fighting strengthened once more the splendid *morale* of the Regiment, and after fresh N.C.O.'s had been made, it was ready again for whatever duty it might be called upon to carry out.

During the afternoon of the 10th a move was made to the north of the Menin Road, and the Gloucesters bivouacked near Bellewaarde Farm, where trenches were dug along the line of a road east of the lake.

At 8.15 a.m. the Corps Reserve—the Gloucesters and Grenadiers—were **11th Nov.** ordered to be ready at short notice to support the 1st Brigade, who were holding the front line from the Menin Road northwards to Polygon Wood. At 10 o'clock definite and urgent instructions were received for them to move to the wood just south-east of Hooge Chateau—the Grenadiers on the right next to the Menin Road, and the Gloucesters to their immediate north. After a three hours' bombardment of unusual intensity, the enemy had commenced a final effort with his *corps d'elite* to break through the British line. Fifteen battalions of the Prussian Guard, with special orders from the Kaiser to break through at all costs, had poured over the shattered remains of the 1st Brigade. Advancing in solid masses through blinding rain and sleet, they swarmed into the woods east of Hooge. Polygon Wood, on their north, remained ours, but Nonne Boschen Wood, further to the west, was entered, and the guns of the 41st R.F.A. Brigade were nearly captured. Supports were, however, available, and the Huns were driven back after reaching what was to be their high-water mark in this First Battle for Ypres.

At 11 a.m. the Gloucesters were again advanced, this time to the cross roads 600 yards south of Westhoek, with the idea of combining with troops of the 2nd Division coming down from the north, and clearing Nonne Boschen Wood of the enemy. Only a small portion of the Battalion actually took part in this counter-attack, but the whole Battalion was ordered up later in the afternoon to take up a new position stretching from Inverness Copse on the south up towards Verbeck Farm, near the south-west corner of Polygon Wood. Here front line trenches were constructed over a frontage of some 400 yards, and were held by the Regiment for four days. The enemy had once more been repulsed, and the pick of his army had been fought to a standstill. The casualties in the Regiment on the 11th amounted to 15—2 killed and 13 wounded.

Between the 12th and the 15th, except for a certain amount of shelling and a few very minor hostile infantry attacks, the line was quiet, and only a few casualties occurred. One N.C.O. and two men wounded, and one man killed. It was during these days that the first German trench mortar bomb or Minenwerfer was encountered, and observed twisting and turning in the air from the opposing trenches. A and D Companies, on the right, were somewhat worried by these new projectiles, but as yet they were not too alarming, and could be dodged to a certain extent.

On the night of the 14th a small party of Camerons sandwiched in between the left of the Gloucesters and the right of the Northamptons, of the 2nd Brigade, were taken out of the line, and their trenches were occupied by the two flanking battalions, strengthened by small parties of reinforcements. Sergeant Crang brought up a draft of 30 men to the Battalion for this task.

Shortly after midnight on the 15th November, the Oxford and Bucks Light Infantry, of the 2nd Division, arrived to relieve the Regiment, and in the early hours of the next day the Gloucesters marched away west, leaving behind them the Salient, with all its horrors and alarms. On the 16th the 3rd Brigade was in Corps Reserve just west of Ypres, but at 4 p.m. the march was continued *via* Vlamertinghe and Ouderdom to the village of Locre, some seven or eight miles from Ypres. Here the Battalion was billeted in the village church for the night. During this day Captain Richmond joined the Regiment after a month's duty at St. Nazaire in connection with the landing of troops at the new Base.

On the 17th, after a march of another seven miles, the Battalion arrived *via* Bailleul at Outtersteen, which was to be its resting place until December 20th. Here a complete reorganisation of the Battalion was carried out, four platoons were formed per company instead of the two which for the last few weeks were all that could be raised, and many N.C.O.'s and men were promoted to complete the establishment.

Whilst at Outtersteen the Regiment was, however, called upon to do one tour of duty—from the 23rd to the 25th November—in the front line, to the immediate right of the French at Petit Bois near Kemmel. Here, although the front line was most exposed,

24th Nov. and could not be reached in daylight, there were fortunately very few casualties. Two men were killed, and two wounded, on the 24th, and two were killed on the night of the 25th/26th, during the relief by the 5th Brigade.

Just under 400 men had joined the Battalion before it went up to Kemmel, and the strength on the 23rd was 9 officers and 752 other ranks. As far as the Gloucestershire Regiment was concerned, the First Battle of Ypres ended on November 16th, when it was relieved from its trenches near Polygon Wood. Of the 26 officers and about 970 men who marched from Poperinghe on October 19th, only Lieutenants Duncan and Morris, and not more than 100 men remained with the Battalion throughout, and marched back from Ypres four weeks later.

The total casualties were as follows:—

	Killed or D. of W.	W'ded.	Prisoners.	Sick.	Total.
Officers ...	10	11	3	1	25
Other Ranks ...	189	413	62	285	949

On the 1st December the Gloucesters were inspected by Sir John French, who congratulated the Regiment, especially on the gallant action of the two platoons at Langemarck on 23rd October. Two days later H.M. the King walked through Outtersteen, and the Battalion lined the road outside the village.

The next ten days or so were spent in training in the vicinity of the village, in route marches, entrenching by night and in practice bomb throwing. On certain days the Brigade was in Army Reserve, and everyone was held in readiness to move at an hour's notice. On the 20th sudden orders were received at about 5 p.m., and the Brigade marched off south some six miles, to Merville. Next morning the Gloucesters, acting as advanced guard to the Brigade, continued the march at 4 a.m., and reached Bethune at about 8 o'clock. Here, after a rest of about 2½ hours, they pushed on again, and soon after midday were in action at Festubert, where trenches lost by the Indian Corps had to be retaken.

An attack with the 1st Brigade on the right, and the 3rd Brigade on the left, was commenced at 3 p.m. The Gloucesters, with A Company leading, formed the right of the 3rd Brigade—on their left were the South Wales Borderers. The ground was waterlogged, and all possible movement was made exceedingly hard. By dark the Battalion had gained about 500 yards, but the losses had been very heavy in proportion. Amongst the officers in A Company, Captain Baynes had been wounded, 2/Lieutenant Danckwerts died as the result of wounds received, and 2/Lieutenant Templer had been taken prisoner. B Company lost 2/Lieutenant Wiggins, died of wounds. In C Company, Captain Pritchett died of wounds, and Lieutenant Seldon was wounded. Captain Bosanquet was also wounded, for the second time during the last six weeks. Amongst the men, 16 were reported killed, 86 wounded, and 94 missing. These figures, when more accurate numbers could be collected at the end of the fighting at Festubert, were, however, slightly reduced, and it is estimated 45 men were killed, 109 wounded, and 4 were taken prisoners.

The attack was to be continued at dawn on the 22nd, but orders for the attack were cancelled, and the Battalion dug in where they were, in the saturated ground, and the Welch came forward on the left to connect up with the South Wales Borderers. During the 22nd, 2/Lieutenant Herbert was fatally wounded.

On the 23rd the trenches were extended and improved as far as possible, but the ghastly state of affairs, together with the cold and wet weather, resulted in an appalling number of men going sick with rheumatism and frostbite. Stretcher bearers were continually at work, and cases were occurring faster than they could be carried away. In the last week of December there must have been nearly 200 of such cases. This was, of course, in the days before the elaborate precautions and preventatives were even thought about.

Fur coats had, however, been issued on the 2nd December, and previous to this H.M. the Queen's gift of body belts had added to the comfort of the men. Greatcoats were naturally always in use, and at this period were buttoned back, after the French fashion, on account of the continual mud and trench work.   **23rd Dec.**

An order was issued at about this time for all officers to wear the men's pattern web equipment, as it had been found that the Sam Brown made them too conspicuous.

Until the end of December, A and B Companies, and C and D Companies, took it in turns to do 48 hours in the trenches, and 48 hours in reserve. Fortunately the situation after the 22nd remained quiet, though 8 men were killed and 10 wounded.

On the 26th the following message was received from the Divisional Commander:—

"The G.O.C. has pleasure in republishing the following congratulatory letter from G.O.C. Corps :—' Sir Douglas Haig wishes to express to the troops his appreciation of the excellent work done by the 1st Division on the 21st and 22nd of December in exceptionally difficult circumstances. The G.O.C. the Division has reported that in this action the following battalions rendered conspicuously gallant services—

2nd Battalion Royal Munster Fusiliers,
2nd Battalion Welch Regiment,
1st Battalion Gloucestershire Regiment,
1st Battalion Coldstream Guards.

Sir D. Haig has read these reports with great pleasure. The 1st Division fully maintained the high reputation which it had already won.'"

On December 31st, Major Gardiner, Captain Foord (to C Company), and Captain Finch (to A Company), joined the 28th from the 2nd Battalion, to help make good the heavy losses in the more senior ranks.

At 6 o'clock in this evening there was an alarm of an attack. This, however, did not materialise, and the Regiment continued to hold the sector in comparative peace, but considerable discomfort, until relieved on 7th January, 1915, by the 17th Lancers of the Indian Corps.

Thus ended the campaign of 1914. With the exception, perhaps, of the Retreat from Mons, the 1st Division had been to the forefront of the fighting, and, as the casualty and honours lists show, the Gloucestershire Regiment took its full share in the struggle for supremacy on the Western Front.

The total casualties amounted to over 1,500—but in spite of these, and the appalling conditions of trench life in France and Flanders in this first winter of the War, the Regiment was one of the few that can boast of never having lost its trenches or having been driven back by the enemy. All through it will be seen any retirement necessary was made in its own good time, and usually on orders from the higher command.

Assuredly a gallant record of a gallant Regiment from a gallant County.

R.M.G.

BATTLE HONOURS AWARDED

MONS.
RETREAT FROM MONS.
MARNE, 1914.
AISNE, 1914.

YPRES, 1914.
LANGEMARCK, 1914.
GHELUVELT.
NONNE BOSSCHEN.

HONOURS AND AWARDS

COMPANION OF THE BATH—
    Lieutenant-Colonel A. C. Lovett.

DISTINGUISHED SERVICE ORDER—
    Major J. O'D. Ingram.
    Captain R. E. Rising.

MILITARY CROSS—
    Lieutenant H. E. de R. Wetherall.
    Lieutenant J. A. L. Caunter.
    Lieutenant D. Baxter.

DISTINGUISHED CONDUCT MEDAL—
    7102 Pte. G. V. Law, D Company.
    7640 Pte. T. H. Orr, D Company.
    5233 Sergt. J. Wilson, D Company.
    8128 Sergt. T. H. Eddy, A Company.
    9360 Sergt. T. J. Knight, A Company.
    6732 Pte. A. E. Crossman, A Company.
    6762 Pte. J. Shipway, Signaller.
    7078 Lce.-Corporal G. Royal, Stretcher Bearer.

MENTIONED IN SIR JOHN FRENCH'S DESPATCHES—

October 8, 1914—
    Lieut.-Colonel A. C. Lovett.
    Captain and Adjutant A. H. Radice.
    2/Lieut. W. F. Watkins (3rd Battalion).
    5506 C.S.M. W. H. Hodges.
    9714 Drummer C. Fluck.
    7102 Pte. G. V. Law.
    7640 Pte. T. H. Orr.

February 18, 1915—
    Captain A. St. J. Blunt.
    Captain R. E. Rising.
    Lieutenant H. E. de R. Wetherall.
    Lieutenant D. Baxter.

February 18, 1915—*continued*.
    4913 C.S.M. A. Long.
    8376 Lce.-Corporal T. New.
    9566 Pte. F. Dutton.
    7951 Pte. A. Faulkes.
    6668 Pte. M. C. Parry.
    7671 Pte. E. C. Robbins.
    9669 Pte. O. J. Taylor.
    7828 Pte. J. Williams.

June 23, 1915—
    Captain G. B. Bosanquet.
    Captain W. P. Pritchett.

OFFICER CASUALTIES

Lieut.-Col. A. C. Lovett	—	To Brigade	Oct. 31st
Major J. O'D. Ingram	—	Wounded	Nov. 7th
Captain A. H. Radice	—	Wounded	Oct. 29th
Major R. M. S. Gardner	—	Killed	Oct. 31st
Captain R. E. Rising	—	Killed	Nov. 7th
Captain W. A. M. Temple	—	Killed	Oct. 21st
Captain G. M. Shipway	—	D. of wounds	Aug. 26th
Captain A. St. J. Blunt	—	Wounded	Nov. 2nd
Captain A. G. McC. Burn	—	Killed	Oct. 29th
Captain N. F. Baynes	—	Sick	Sept.
Lieut. F. H. McL. Young	—	Wounded	Oct. 21st
Lieut. H. E. de R. Wetherall	—	Wounded	Oct. 29th
Lieut. J. A. L. Caunter	—	Sick	Sept. 1st
Lieut. M. W. Halford	—	Wounded	Nov. 7th
Lieut. D. Duncan	—	—	—
Lieut. R. K. Swanick	—	Killed	Sept. 15th
2/Lieut. B. F. R. Davis	—	Wounded	Sept. 17th
2/Lieut. A. D. Harding	—	Killed	Oct. 29th
2/Lieut. W. S. Yalland	—	Killed	Oct. 23rd
2/Lieut. D. Baxter	—	Wounded	Oct. 23rd
2/Lieut. R. M. Grazebrook	—	Sick	Sept. 13th
2/Lieut. Hon. N. F. Somerset	—	Wounded	Sept. 15th
2/Lieut. M. Kershaw	—	Killed	Nov. 7th
2/Lieut. H. E. Hippisley	—	Killed	Oct. 23rd
2/Lieut. W. F. Watkins	—	Wounded	Sept. 26th
Lieut. and Q.M. W. J. Hewitt	—	—	—
Captain A. A McLeod	Sept. 5th	Killed	Nov. 2nd
Captain A. Capel	Sept. 8th	Wounded	Oct. 21st
*Lieut. J. A. L. Caunter	Sept. 21st	Prisoner	Oct. 31st
Lieut. C. D'A. S. Bush	Sept. 20th	Wounded	Oct. 31st
2/Lieut. D. A. Greenslade	Sept. 25th	Prisoner	Oct. 29th
2/Lieut. T. R. A. Morris	Oct. 4th	—	—
2/Lieut. J. F. L. Hartmann	Oct. 4th	Sick	Oct. 27th
Lieut. J. H. L. Scott-Tucker	Oct. 19th	Wounded	Oct. 31st
2/Lieut. H. K. Foster	Oct. 19th	Killed	Oct. 29th
Captain A. F. Chapman	Oct. 28th	Prisoner	Oct. 29th
*2/Lieut. R. M. Grazebrook	Nov. 1st	Wounded	Nov. 2nd
Captain W. P. Pritchett	Nov. 3rd	D. of wounds	Dec. 21st
Captain G. B. Bosanquet	Nov. 8th	Wounded	Dec. 21st
*Captain A. St. J. Blunt	Nov. 8th	—	—
Captain H. C. Richmond	Nov. 16th	Killed	1915
*Captain N. F. Baynes	Nov. 21st	Wounded	Dec. 21st
2/Lieut. M. C. W. Herbert	Nov. 18th	D. of wounds	Dec. 21st
2/Lieut. C. F. L. Templer	Nov. 18th	Prisoner	Dec. 21st
2/Lieut. N. Durrant	Nov. 28th	Sick	1915
2/Lieut. E. C. Walters	Nov. 28th	Killed	Dec. 21st
Captain A. J. Menzies	Nov. 29th	England	1915
2/Lieut. L. C. Brown	Nov. 29th	Sick	1915
2/Lieut. D. H. Wiggin	Nov. 29th	D. of wounds	Dec. 21st

2/Lieut. A. Seldon	Dec. 3rd	Sick	—
2/Lieut. R. W. Danckwert	Dec. 3rd	Killed	Dec. 21st
2/Lieut. R. A. Angier	Dec. 9th	Sick	Dec. 27th
2/Lieut. A. A. Vere	Dec. 9th	—	—
2/Lieut. A. R. Phillpots	Nov. 28th	—	—
*2/Lieut. Hon. N. F. Somerset	Dec. 14th	Wounded	1915
2/Lieut. G. C. Firbank	Dec. 15th	Wounded	1915
Major G. F. Gardiner	Dec. 31st	Sick	1915
Captain W. P. S. Foord	Dec. 31st	Wounded	1915
Captain F. C. Finch	Dec. 31st	Wounded	1915

Total, 59.

Killed, 17.   Wounded, 16.   Prisoner, 3.   Sick, 5.

* Rejoined.

REINFORCEMENTS

No. of Reinforcement.	Officer.	N.C.O.'s	O.R's	Total.	Date of Embarkation.
Battalion	26	94	877	971	13th August
1st	Capt. McLeod	4	94	98	22nd August
2nd	Capt. Capel	2	91	93	26th August
3rd	Lieut. C. Bush	2	91	93	4th September
4th	Lieut. Morris	2	159	161	12th September
5th	Lieut. Hartmann	2	91	93	20th September
6th	Capt. Bosanquet	2	18	20	3rd October
7th	Officer of K.R.R.	6	284	290	11th November
8th	Major Menzies	1	79	80	23rd November
9th	Lieut. Seldon	3	97	100	28th November
10th	Lieut. Somerset	6	134	140	2nd December

CASUALTIES DURING 1914

	CASUALTIES.										DRAFTS.	
	OFFICERS.				OTHER RANKS.				TOTAL.			
	K.	W.	P.	S.	K.	W.	P.	S.	O.	O.R's.	O.	O.R's.
Retreat—												
Aug. 13	–	–	–	–	–	–	–	–			26	971
,, 26	1	–	–	–	6	25	7	–				
,, 28	–	–	–	–	1	–	–	–				
,, 30	–	–	–	–	–	1	–	–				
Sept. 3	–	–	–	–	–	–	1	–				
	1	–	–	2	7	26	8	85*	3	126		
Aisne—												
Sept. 5	–	–	–	–	–	–	–	–			1	93
,, 6	–	–	–	–	1	2	–	–				
,, 8	–	–	–	–	–	–	–	–			1	90
,, 9	–	–	–	–	–	1	–	–				
,, 14	1	1	–	–	14	87	–	–				
,, 16	–	–	–	–	6	7	–	–				
,, 17	–	1	–	–	–	2	–	–				
,, 18	–	–	–	–	–	4	–	–				
,, 19	–	–	–	–	–	7	–	–				
,, 20	–	–	–	–	1	7	–	–			1	96
,, 21	–	–	–	–	–	1	–	–			1	10
,, 22	–	–	–	–	1	6	–	–				
,, 23	–	–	–	–	–	1	–	–				
,, 24	–	–	–	–	1	1	–	–				
,, 25	–	–	–	–	–	1	–	–			1	–
,, 26	–	1	–	–	4	19	–	–				
,, 27	–	–	–	–	1	4	–	–				
,, 30	–	–	–	–	–	2	–	–			2	–
Oct. 4	–	–	–	–	–	–	–	–				
,, 7	–	–	–	–	–	2	–	–				
	1	3	–	1	29	154	–	56*	5	239		
Ypres—												
Oct. 19	–	–	–	–	–	–	–	–			2	51
,, 21	1	3	–	–	12	36	–	–				
,, 22	–	–	–	–	5	12	–	–				
,, 23	2	1	–	–	13	45	–	–				
,, 27	–	–	–	–	–	5	–	–			1	70
,, 28	–	–	–	–	–	–	–	–				
,, 29	3	2	2	–	52	70	39	–				
,, 30	–	–	–	–	5	5	–	–				
,, 31	1	2	1	–	15	45	5	–				
Carried forward	7	8	3	–	102	218	44	–				

	CASUALTIES.								TOTAL.		DRAFTS.	
	OFFICERS.				OTHER RANKS.				O.	O.R's.	O.	O.R's.
	K.	W.	P.	S.	K.	W.	P.	S.				
Ypres—*(contd.)*												
Brought forward	7	8	3	–	102	218	44	–				
Nov. 1	–	–	–	–	17	43	10	–			1	49
,, 2	1	2	–	–	10	48	4	–				
,, 3	–	–	–	–	–	6	–	–			1	200
,, 4	–	–	–	–	2	9	–	–				
,, 5	–	–	–	–	13	29	–	–				
,, 7	2	2	–	–	36	47	8	–				
,, 8	–	–	–	–	–	–	–	–			2	20
,, 10	–	–	–	–	–	2	–	–				
,, 11	–	–	–	–	2	13	–	–				
,, 12	–	–	–	–	1	1	–	–				
,, 13	–	–	–	–	–	–	–	–			–	30
,, 15	–	–	–	–	–	2	–	–				
	10	12	3	1	183	418	66	81*	26	748		
Kemmel—												
Nov. 16	–	–	–	–	–	–	–	–			1	43
,, 18	–	–	–	–	–	–	–	–			2	300*
,, 21	–	–	–	–	–	–	–	–			1	12
,, 24	–	–	–	–	2	2	–	–				
,, 25	–	–	–	–	2	–	–	–				
,, 28	–	–	–	–	–	–	–	–			3	–
,, 29	–	–	–	–	–	–	–	–			3	10
Dec. 3	–	–	–	–	–	–	–	–			2	–
,, 9	–	–	–	–	–	–	–	–			2	–
,, 14	–	–	–	–	–	–	–	–			1	–
,, 15	–	–	–	–	–	–	–	–			1	20*
	–	–	–	–	4	2	–	10*	–	16		
Festubert—												
Dec. 21	5	2	1	–	45	109	4	–				
,, 25	–	–	–	–	1	–	–	–				
,, 26	–	–	–	–	1	–	–	–				
,, 27	–	–	–	–	1	–	–	–				
,, 28	–	–	–	–	1	2	–	–				
,, 29	–	–	–	–	1	5	–	–				
,, 30	–	–	–	–	1	1	–	–				
,, 31	–	–	–	–	2	2	–	–			3	–
	5	2	1	1	53	119	4	228*	9	404		
Total	17	17	4	5	276	719	78	464*	43	1,533	59	2,065

* Approximate only.

Table to show the Percentage of Casualties suffered by the men who actually embarked with the Battalion in August, 1914:—

August and September—
Killed, Died of Wounds, Died	3.6	
Wounded, Injured	17.6	
Prisoner	.8	30.1%
Sick	8.1	
Promoted (?)	.2	

October—
Killed, etc.	6.7	
Wounded	14.2	
Prisoner	2.4	24.6%
Sick	1.3	
(?)	.2	

November—
Killed, etc.	4.3	
Wounded	10.6	17.9%
Prisoner	.8	
Sick	2.2	

December—
Killed, etc.	1.5	
Wounded	2.6	6.6%
Prisoner	.3	
Sick	2.2	

Remained with Battalion until—
1915	13.4%
1916	3.0%
1917	1.0%
1918	1.3%
1919	1.5%

2nd BATTALION
THE GLOUCESTERSHIRE REGIMENT
"YPRES, 1915"

2nd BATTALION
THE GLOUCESTERSHIRE REGIMENT
"YPRES 1915"

COMING home, as it did, from China in November, 1914, the 2nd Battalion of the Gloucestershire Regiment formed part of the 27th Division, under Major-General T. D'O. Snow. This division consisted mostly of battalions from the outlying garrisons of Asia and the Mediterranean. The 81st Brigade (Brigadier-General Macfarlane) was composed of the 1/Royal Scots, 2/Gloucesters, 2/Cameron Highlanders, 1/Argyll and Sutherland Highlanders, 9/Royal Scots and the 9/Argylls, the two latter battalions being Territorials.

On December 18th the 61st embarked at Southampton for France, and by the 10th January, 1915, were in the line some 3 miles south of Ypres, in the vicinity of Dickebusch. Here, and at St. Eloi, a few miles further east, nearly two months were spent learning the job of trench warfare, and, incidentally, suffering many discomforts and several casualties from the cold and mud, in addition to those from the minor tactical operations carried out.

The following officers had embarked with the Battalion for France, and on the next page are given the names of those who joined in the Dickebusch area, and before the actual Second Battle of Ypres commenced.

Lieut.-Col. G. S. Tulloh (Commanding).
Major R. Conner (2nd in Command).
Major G. F. Gardiner - - - - To 1st Batt., Dec. 30, '14.
Major F. C. Nisbet.
Captain D. Burges.
Captain D. J. B. McMahon - - - Frostbite, Jan 29, '15.
Captain H. B. Spear.
Captain W. P. S. Foord - - - - To 1st Batt., Dec. 30, '14.
Captain F. C. Finch - - - - To 1st Batt., Dec. 30, '14.
Captain A. C. Vicary (Adjutant).
Captain E. G. H. Power.
Lieut. C. E. Gardner.
Lieut. D. K. Garnier - - - - Frostbite, Feb. 19, '15.
Lieut. L. A. W. D. Lachlan - - - Wounded, Feb. 5, '15.
Lieut. W. H. Parkinson - - - - Frostbite, Feb. 19, '15.
Lieut. J. B. Smalley - - - - Wounded, Feb. 20, '15.
Lieut. C. S. W. Greenland.
Lieut. L. H. Cox.
Lieut. B. A. Capel Cure - - - - Sick, March 29, '15.
Lieut. E. D'O. Aplin.
Lieut. W. G. Chapman.
2/Lieut. H. Rummins - - - - Sick, March 22, '15.
2/Lieut. R. J. Croft - - - - Killed, March 21, '15.
2/Lieut. F. C. Basdell - - - - Wounded, Jan. 17, '15.
Lieut. & Q.M. E. H. Dinham.
Lieut. H. B. Sherlock (R.A.M.C.).

1st April Joined later—
    2/Lieut. F. Steele (3/Essex, Jan. 21).
    2/Lieut. A. G. Blake (3/Essex, Jan. 21) - - Wounded, Feb. 4, '15.
    Lieut. H. M. Harrison (R. of O., Jan. 28) - - Killed, March 19, '15.
    2/Lieut F. H. Toop (Feb. 17).
    Capt. W. V. Churchill-Longman (3 Bn., Feb. 21).
    2/Lieut. S. Barker (3rd Bn., March 1).
    2/Lieut. F. McC. Rawlins (3rd Bn., March 13).
    2/Lieut. T. H. Cordes (3rd Bn., March 13).
    Major D. J. B. McMahon (Rejoined, March 17).
    Lieut. R. M. Grazebrook (March 28).

A number of these had already become casualties by the time the march to Ypres was ordered, and on 1st April, 1915, the actual distribution was as follows:—

   BATTALION HEADQUARTERS—
        Lieut.-Colonel Tulloh (Commanding Officer).
        Major Conner (Second in Command).
        Captain A. C. Vicary (Adjutant).
        Lieut. Gardner (Transport Officer).
        Lieut. Cox (Machine Gun Officer).
        Lieut. Dinham (Quarter-Master).
        Lieut. Sherlock (Medical Officer).

   A COMPANY—
        Captain Spear.
        Lieut. W. G. Chapman.
        2/Lieut. Cordes.
        2/Lieut. Rawlins.

   B COMPANY—
        Major Nisbet.
        Capt. Churchill-Longman.
        Lieut. Aplin.
        2/Lieut. Steele.

   C COMPANY—
        Captain D. Burges.
        Captain E. G. H. Power.
        Lieut. Greenland.

   D COMPANY—
        Captain McMahon.
        Lieut. Grazebrook.
        2/Lieut. Barker.

On the 4th April, Easter Day, orders were received for the 81st Brigade to march *via* Vlamertinghe to Ypres, and to join the rest of the 27th Division in the Salient, where they were taking over a sector from the French.

The railway station at Ypres was reached at about 7.30 in the evening, and it was then learnt that the original destination of the Regiment, some huts near Potije, was still occupied by French troops, and that, while C and D Companies were to push on to relieve certain French supporting troops near the Ypres-Roulers railway, the rest of the Battalion were to billet in Ypres itself. The town had as yet suffered very little from hostile bombardment. It was certainly shelled each night, but civilians were still carrying on their trades there, and many troops were quartered in the place. Whilst there the Battalion had no casualties, and were lucky in getting good billets.

C and D Companies, proceeding along the Roulers road as far as Potije, **4th April** turned south near the village, and eventually, by about midnight, had relieved some French troops—the former company in Nonne Bosschen Wood, and the latter near Bellewaarde Lake. April 5th and 6th were spent mostly in cleaning up the débris left by the predecessors, and in getting the bearings of the new sector. Officers were sent up to reconnoitre the front line trenches which were to be occupied in the near future. Some of these could only be approached under cover of darkness, as in these early days communication trenches were rather the exception than the rule.

On the 6th 2/Lieut. Brennan, 3rd Battalion, joined the Battalion with a draft of 42 men. He was posted to C Company. On this day also, 2/Lieut. Toop was wounded whilst on a reconnaissance.

On the following day the rest of the Battalion marched out of Ypres along the Menin Road, and took over dug-outs and shelters from the French in Glencorse Wood, while C and D Companies moved south across the Menin Road and into shelters in Sanctuary Wood.

At 7.30 p.m. on the 8th the Regiment moved up for its first tour of duty in the Salient, and relieved the Royal Irish Fusiliers, of the 82nd Brigade. The actual frontage stretched from the S.E. corner of Shrewsbury Forest, on the right, along the valley of the Bassevillebeek, and along the eastern edge of the Herenthage Chateau grounds as far as the chateau itself. A, B and D Companies moved into the front line, while Battalion Headquarters and three platoons of C Company went into dug-outs in Bodmin Copse. The fourth platoon of C Company, together with the Regimental Snipers, some machine gunners and stretcher bearers, took up their quarters in the cellars of a large semi-ruined white chateau, just east of Hooge village, and south of the Menin Road, called "Stirling Castle."

After taking over the trenches it was found that they were a second line system, the French having lost the front line some time before. This the French had failed to inform the British troops when they took over, and the primitive trench maps were naturally the cause of many troubles. Old communication trenches were found to lead right into the then German front line! For the most part, however, the actual trenches occupied by the Regiment were good, chiefly built up as breastworks owing to the wet ground, and that portion which was in Herenthage Wood could be got at by day. On the right, however, owing to the communication trenches being uncompleted, the line was isolated during daylight. The opposing lines were roughly 70 yards apart on either side of the Bassevillebeek stream, and it was only from the slopes in rear that the German system could be watched. Here the snipers used to lie up to observe and report upon all enemy movements.

After an uneventful tour the Gloucesters were relieved in the evening of the 12th by the 1/Argylls, who usually took a turn in and out with the Regiment. Billets were obtained in Ypres, and during the first night there the place was visited by a Zeppelin. It was found, also, that the town had been much knocked about during the last few days, though a number of shops and the market were still being run.

There was at this time a general feeling that something big was in the wind. Rumours were flying about, and occasional alarms occurred whereby everyone stood to. The Canadian Division marched through *en route* for St. Julian, and other fresh troops had begun to arrive in the locality to relieve the much-tried original Expeditionary Force. At this period the dispositions of the Allied forces in the neighbourhood of Ypres were as follows :—

Belgian Army	-	Nieuport—Woumen.
A French Army	-	Woumen—Langemarck (45th Colonial Division on their right).

16th April   British II Army—
    Canadian Corps:
        1st Div.   Langemarck—North of Zonnebeke.
    V Corps:
        28th Div.   N.E. of Zonnebeke—S.E. of Polygon Wood.
        27th Div.   Polygon Wood—E. of Veldhoek—N. of Hill 60.
    II Corps:
        2nd Div.   Hill 60—St. Eloi.
        3rd Div.   Wytschaete—Messines.
    III Corps—
        4th & 6th Divs.—
                    South to Bois Grenier.

At 9 p.m. on the 16th April the Battalion marched back along the Menin Road and relieved the Argylls in the same trenches. This time B Company was the company in support in Bodmin Copse.

During the next day it was learnt that an attack was to be made by the 5th Division to the right of the 27th Division sector, to gain possession of a small knoll near Zwartelen, which was of great value as an observation post to whichever side was holding it. At about 7 p.m. mines were exploded under the hill, and "Hill 60" was captured, though there was very serious fighting to retain possession of it then and in the future. During the operation the Gloucesters, together with the other units in the line at the time, kept up bursts of rapid fire with a view of keeping the enemy on the jump.

On the following day, the 18th, the Battalion made its first acquaintance with "Minny"—the German Minenwerfer or trench-mortar. Several of the sausage-shaped bombs were hurled over into the trenches of C Company, on the right. Luckily they could be fairly easily observed twisting and turning over and over in the air, and could usually be avoided. Unfortunately on one occasion a man stumbled and blocked the way for others, and several casualties occurred. During the morning of this day, also, Lieut. Brenan was killed by a German sniper whilst supervising the rebuilding of a breach in the parapet. This officer was less than twenty years old, and had only been out in the country for a few days.

The remainder of the four days' tour passed off quietly, though the woods in the vicinity were shelled at odd times.

At 1 a.m. on the 21st the Argylls arrived to take over, and the Battalion marched back to shelters in Sanctuary Wood under unpleasantly close and accurate shell fire.

Heavy fighting continued round about Hill 60, and, amongst others, the Camerons, of the 81st Brigade, had been sent over to the right as supports. As a result of this the 1/Royal Scots, in the line to the left of the Gloucesters, had not been relieved. To enable the Royal Scots to get some rest, the Gloucesters were ordered to relieve them in the evening of the 22nd. At about 6.30 p.m. on that day a tremendous bombardment was heard to commence away to the north. At the same time Sanctuary Wood came in for a minor shelling, with the result that all communication with Brigade Headquarters and the Royal Scots was cut off. The Battalion was therefore without orders or information, and the relief was necessarily hung up for the time. What had happened was that the Hun had launched his first gas attack in the neighbourhood of Langemarck at a point where the Canadian Division's left linked up with the Colonial troops of the Frency Army. Under the awful conditions those Turcos who remained alive broke, the left of the Canadians was destroyed, and a huge gap of some five miles was formed in the Allied line. Fortunately the enemy himself appeared at a loss, afraid to take full advantage of his successes. Gradually British reinforcements began to arrive, odd battalions, single companies, or even smaller units, and the line, though driven in, held firm.

At about 2.45 a.m. on the morning after, the 23rd, orders were received for the relief of the Royal Scots to be carried out at once, and for the Regiment to march to Inverness

Copse by companies to take over. When approaching the woods and crossing the Menin Road, the attention of the enemy must have been attracted, as there was a period of very heavy machine gun fire directed against the area in which the Battalion was moving. By lying absolutely flat, the shots went high, and no casualties were suffered. By this time, however, it was getting light, and the colonel of the Royal Scots thinking he would be unable to get back without being seen, refused to be relieved, and the Gloucesters returned to Sanctuary Wood. The Royal Scots actually remained in the line 34 days during this tour of duty.

23rd April

At about 11 a.m. the Battalion had orders to "stand to," and later were moved up into the second line trenches along the eastern edge of Sanctuary Wood. After a short period they were, however, sent back, not being required. At this time the supporting lines were most primitive, and in many places non-existent. Working parties were constantly out during the nights digging trenches, wiring and preparing barricades for the main road.

April 24th was the first of several days of continual alarms and moves. In the early afternoon the Regiment got sudden orders to move off to the north, to support the Canadians. The enemy had apparently attacked again under cover of clouds of gas, and in spite of vigorous counter-attacks, had driven back the left of the Canadian Division. Previous to this move two companies of the Gloucesters were being held in readiness to march south to reinforce the 82nd Brigade, and officers had reconnoitred the route. Now, however, the whole Battalion marched off as rapidly as possible over the open country towards Potije. Near the Ypres-Roulers railway were several British and Belgian batteries in action, and at one point two 4.7 in. guns were seen in a hedgerow, side by side, and each facing exactly opposite directions—so narrow was the salient. The enemy naturally were replying to the Allied fire, and the march in artillery formation to Potije was most unpleasant, and resulted in several casualties. It must be remembered that this was the disastrous period of the shortage of shells, and it was a very rare thing for the British guns to be heard really attempting to deal with the hostile bombardments.

Canadian wounded and asphyxiated men were streaming back, and sundry small units were moving up to reinforce. The Battalion was not, however, called upon, and by 7 p.m. returned to its shelters in Sanctuary Wood.

Up to this period there had been no preparations for gas warfare, and men were ordered to tie socks, etc., soaked in urine over their mouths whenever they had the yellow chlorine gas clouds against them. Soon small cotton wool pads were issued for this purpose, and after a few more days the more efficient cotton-waste and gauze respirators chemically treated. These remained in use until the flannel smoke-helmet with a mica eyepiece was issued at the end of May.

On the 25th April, B Company, under Major Nisbet, was detached to Bellewaarde Farm, to support and carry for the 80th Brigade. The next day this company were ordered up to the N.W. corner of Polygon Wood to dig communication trenches for the support line. This work was unfortunately spotted by a German observation balloon, and twice artillery fire was opened on the party. Their dug-outs at the edge of Bellewaarde Lake were also bombarded with tear shells. At another time this company had to continue trenches about Verbeck Farm, the scene of the Prussian Guard attack near Nonne Bosschen Wood, in November of the previous year.

Meanwhile the rest of the Battalion once more marched off to Potije, but again were not needed. This time the fighting in the north resulted in the 28th Division being driven back from the Gravenstafel Ridge, in spite of their being reinforced by the Northumbrian Territorial Division and the Lahore Indian Division.

On the evening of the 28th, B Company rejoined the Regiment, and on the following evening A Company and half C Company went up to the trenches to take over a portion of the Royal Scots line, to enable them to work a system of company reliefs.

29th April The portion now held by the Gloucesters was about Herenthage Chateau, to the immediate south of the Menin Road. The chateau building itself was half in British hands and half in the enemy's. One small post was on an island on the Dumbarton Lakes, and could only be reached by one man at a time at night on a sort of raft. The rest of the Battalion was kept busy these days in making dug-outs and shelters in Zouave Wood for the Camerons, who were expected back from Hill 60, and in digging reserve trenches for the 80th Brigade to the north, and the 82nd Brigade to the south.

April 30th saw the arrival of Captain M. W. Halford (posted to A Company) and a new type of trench mortar. This latter was a stage more elaborate and more safe than the original drain pipe affair, in that it had a rifle body fixed to the base to enable the charge to be fired by a special cartridge.

Further hostile attacks, accompanied by gas, were made daily, chiefly about St. Julien and Verlorenhoek, and the time had come when the Salient was all but cut off. Partly for fear of this, and partly to economise troops, it was decided on the 2nd May that it would be necessary to withdraw the whole of the eastern end of the Salient to, in the centre, a distance of $2\frac{1}{4}$ miles. The actual withdrawal was to be carried out during the night of the 3rd/4th May. The new front line was to be an old French subsidiary line, very weak and very incomplete. Orders were, however, issued for work to be commenced at once, and digging and wiring were carried out all the 2nd and 3rd.

In the Battalion sector, which stretched roughly some 600 yards south of the Menin Road, the new line was situated along the eastern edge of Sanctuary Wood, about half a mile in rear of the old line. The right of the sector was bounded by a track leading S.E. towards Bodmin Copse, and the left rested on a track running from Sanctuary Wood to Stirling Castle. About halfway along this frontage the wood formed a right angle pointing E.S.E. towards the enemy. At the apex of this, and on slightly higher ground, was an old French O.P., and a short line of trench. This was connected by two communication trenches with the new main line which cut off the corner of the wood. Sanctuary Wood at this time was already the worse for shell fire, much of the undergrowth had gone, and many large trees were lying in a tangled mass in all directions. In front, and stretching to the east towards Stirling Castle, and to the south towards Bodmin Copse, lay open rolling fields mostly covered by wild mustard some two or three feet high, and affording excellent cover for enemy patrols, or even for larger bodies of men. The wire out in front was the remains of the old French " crinoline " wire, hastily improved and strengthened with coils of barbed wire.

To B Company, under Major Nisbet, was allotted the right half of this new sector, whilst D Company, under Captain McMahon, were responsible for the left, and for the advanced post. One machine gun was also placed in the advanced post, whilst the other was positioned on the left of B Company. A and C Companies were to go in support some 200 yards to the rear, in dug-outs with Battalion Headquarters.

The withdrawal to this new system was carried out with success during the night of 3rd/4th May. Although it involved the whole of the 27th, and half of the 28th Divisions, and effected in many cases from positions within a few yards of the enemy, not a man or a gun was lost in the operation. In the Battalion area B and D Companies were in their new positions by 9 p.m. on the 3rd, with half of C Company in a covering position about Stirling Castle, about halfway between the old and new trenches. At 10.30 p.m. half the men from the forward line withdrew, bringing back all spare ammunition and stores. At midnight the remainder crept quietly back, only leaving one or two men to fire an occasional round and to send up flares. These men, in their turn, retired at about 12.15 a.m. The enemy here, as elsewhere, appears to have been ignorant of the move, and did not discover about it until some two hours after it had been completed. Actually opposite the Gloucesters the Germans continued their usual sniping practices, and it was not until 6 a.m. on the morning of the 4th that the 61st snipers reported the enemy advancing in twos and threes, and apparently unarmed. Some appeared to be wearing khaki uniforms, though in the early morning mist and rain it was hard to make anything definite out. The snipers opened fire, and the enemy that remained doubled back to the woods. About this time more firing commenced on the right from the direction of Bodmin Copse, and owing to enfilade fire all the advanced observation posts had to fall back on the main line. **4th May**

From 7 a.m. onwards small parties of the enemy appeared amongst the trees round Stirling Castle, and more especially on the high ground to the left of the Chateau. Here they were seen to be busy getting under cover and digging or improving trenches along the western edge of the chateau grounds. In many cases this was the first occasion that men of the 2nd Battalion had really seen a Bosche, and there was considerable excitement and eagerness to get a shot. Several of the enemy were hit, and were seen to be dragged back into safety. The range was about 600-700 yards.

Bodmin Copse was also occupied by the Germans, and parties could be seen doubling out and starting to dig a new line some hundreds of yards in front. What appeared to be a light gun or trench mortar was also spotted on the forward edge of Bodmin Copse. Through glasses the German gunners could be seen hastily digging it in, and building up a sandbag protection. So short, however, were the British gunners of ammunition, that no attempt to knock it out could be made.

At about 10.30 a.m. the enemy started shelling the line, mostly with light " whizz bang " shrapnel, and the advanced post, being very conspicuous at the corner of the wood, came in for most of the trouble. At this time D Company had three platoons up in the advanced trenches, and one platoon in support in the main line. Company Headquarters was in a dug-out at the very apex of the wood. During the shelling most of the men were got back to the main line, which, owing to the shape of the ground and to the trees, was more sheltered. In the future, also, the advanced trench was only lightly held by day, and reinforced from the main trench at night. After this bombardment, and probably owing to there being no effective reply, the enemy, no doubt thinking it was only a temporary British position, started to push on. A few of them, under cover of their artillery fire, had actually advanced in the mustard to about one hundred yards of D Company's forward position. These men were easily dealt with, and the rest crept away again to their new line.

At about 2.30 p.m. a fresh bombardment was commenced, but this time it consisted of many largish H.E. shells, which made a nasty mess amongst the trees, though they mostly burst between the two lines of D Company. In spite of practically evacuating their forward line, this company had several casualties, and Captain McMahon was wounded himself, though not seriously enough to necessitate his leaving the company. B Company in the right sector saw nothing of the enemy, and were not worried by the shelling.

That night passed quietly, the enemy no doubt too busy digging in and improving his new positions to do any serious trouble.

At 5 a.m. on the 5th the bombardment recommenced, and very considerable damage was done in D Company's trenches. For the most part it was light artillery being used, but a number of heavy " Crumps " came over, and burst some 50 feet up, with great greasy yellow clouds of smoke and fumes. The company headquarter dug-out received 13 direct hits, and was entirely shattered. Luckily the occupants, Captain McMahon, Lieutenant Grazebrook, and an artillery bombardier (doing observation work) got away to the right, and succeeded in getting the surviving men back to the main line, where the shell fire was less heavy. The machine gun in the advanced position was put out of action, and except for an observation post near the telephone dug-out on the extreme right of the forward line, this corner of the wood was entirely vacated.

At about 11.15 the bombardment slackened, but at 12 noon it recommenced with renewed vigour. At 2 p.m. an observer from the front rushed back to say the Germans were attacking, and the company hastened to man the front trench. This, however, proved to be a false alarm, only a few of the enemy having been spotted doubling over the open some 400 yards to the right front.

5th May   At about 2.30 p.m. the shelling ceased, and a survey of the damage done could be made. This was appalling. In many places the parapet had been absolutely blown away, and in others the trench was almost filled with débris and fallen trees. Some thirty men of D Company had been hit. Those who could walk went off to the dressing station in rear of Sanctuary Wood. Others were carried off by the stretcher bearers who could now get forward. The dead were taken back to be buried at night. The telephone wires back to Battalion Headquarters had naturally been cut. These were now mended, and information filtered back. Captain McMahon had been wounded in the head a second time, and was sent back.

At 1 p.m. the following message was received from Brigade Headquarters : " Enemy have reached 5th Division, Hill 60, under cover of asphyxiating gas, and are using it against our trenches. Warn all men to keep respirators wet." Later, at about 5 p.m., information was received that the Germans had penetrated the 15th Brigade's line on the right of the 27th Division, and were also reported to be cutting the wire in front of the 82nd Brigade. Enemy's aircraft had been busy throughout the day. Once again B Company had been lucky, and their trenches had been very little damaged, though A Company's dug-outs in rear had been badly knocked about.

At 9.30 p.m. C and A Companies arrived to take over from D and B respectively. The relief was very slow, owing to the guides losing themselves, and to the terrible state of the communication trenches. The relief was completed at about 1.30 a.m. the following morning.

May 6th was another day of bombardment, though not of such a severe character as on the previous day. The enemy's snipers also became busy, while their front line troops could be seen sapping out across No Man's Land.

At about 3.10 a.m. on the 7th, very heavy rifle and artillery fire was opened on the Camerons' trenches, to the left of C Company, and this spread along to the Battalion frontage, but ceased about 4 a.m. At 10 a.m. the line and dug-outs behind were again shelled, but the British guns this day were able to make some effective reply. The enemy continued to sap towards the British line, and each morning found a new trench some twenty to fifty yards nearer.

May 8th commenced more lively, and at 6.45 a.m. heavy shelling recommenced on the forward line occupied by C Company. Some little time later it was learned that the enemy had broken through at Bellewaarde Lake, but had subsequently been driven back. After an hour's pause the bombardment started again at noon, and C Company were badly knocked about. They had had about 45 men hit, Lieutenant Greenland had been killed and Lieutenant Cox wounded. At about 3.15 p.m., so serious had things become up in front, that Lieutenant-Colonel Tulloh decided to reinforce the main line. B Company was sent up to support the left, and D Company to the second line, while two companies of the Leinsters (82nd Brigade) were brought up as a reserve.

At about 4.30 p.m. the shelling slackened somewhat, and the supports were able to be withdrawn. In the evening, at 9.45 p.m., the two companies in front were relieved, C Company by B on the left, and A Company by D on the right. Digging was continued throughout the night, which otherwise passed off quietly. At about 6.30 a.m. the next morning, however, May 9th, the enemy opened a terrific artillery fire on the front trenches of the Battalion. Two " whizz-bang " guns were particularly dangerous with enfilade fire from the right. In reply to this bombardment, again the British artillery was almost powerless. Much of the available ammunition, besides guns, had been sent south to take part in the I Army attack on the Aubers Ridge. Lack of ammunition and lack of observation posts also, made any effective reply difficult. One Belgian battery was close behind the Battalion frontage, and inspired confidence by firing salvos. A couple of 4.7's, though they now and again dropped a shell in the Gloucesters' sector, did as best they could.

The first shelling was directed on the forward trench, where three platoons of B Company were situated. It lasted for ten minutes, and was followed by fifteen minutes of very heavy rifle fire. After this there was another ten minutes' bombardment, again followed by intense rifle and machine gun fire. As the result of the shelling, great damage was done to the forward trenches, and it was found the three platoons in front were completely cut off. Major Nisbet, therefore, ordered all but ten men per platoon to try and get back to the main line in rear. The succession of ten minutes' shelling and fifteen minutes' rifle fire made life a perfect hell, and movement of any kind was practically impossible. Finding his part of the forward trench quite untenable, Lieutenant Aplin, though seriously wounded at the time, succeeded in getting back the three surviving men with him to the main line. On his right Sergeant Coopey, with a few men of a machine gun post, was quite cut off after the third bombardment.

At about this time, 7.15 a.m., the enemy attacked from Stirling Castle, and from the right front. Heavy fire was opened on them by Sergeant Ball's platoon, and the machine gun, but the enemy succeeded in gaining the trenches and communication trench of the forward position. A number of men of B Company succeeded in getting back from the forward trench, but very many were knocked out or buried. Major Nisbet, himself, with Captain Churchill-Longman and some 29 men and two machine guns, were at the time near the telephone dug-out on the right of the forward line. The enemy were now pouring into the left portion, and were digging in and bringing up machine guns. Their losses at this period were very great, and were estimated at 350 killed. Major Nisbet's party manned the shattered parapets, and opened fire to the south and east, but the Germans succeeded in getting behind them, and astride the communication trench. Luckily there was a circular bit of trench round a bump in the ground in the centre. This proved to be defensible, chiefly because the slight rise prevented the men being hit in the back. Casualties, however, mounted up, and one machine gun was put out of action by a German officer with a revolver. He and many others were knocked out, but their reinforcements kept coming in from the corner of the wood.

The first word of this attack reached Battalion Headquarters by runner at about 7.30 a.m., the telephone and wire all having been destroyed earlier by shell fire. The support company, A Company, under the command of the Second in Command, Major Conner, was rushed up into the main trench to meet the attack. At the same time C Company moved up from in reserve, and with Battalion Headquarters occupied the partially formed second line some 250 yards in rear of the main trench. Two companies of the Leinsters were also sent up in support.

Major Conner appears to have pushed ahead of the supporting company, and to have attempted to advance along the communication trench leading to the left of the advanced position. This, of course, was by then in the hands of the enemy, and Major Conner must have walked straight into them. He and the few men behind him were all killed or taken prisoners. Major Conner, himself, was wounded and taken. He was repatriated on account of ill-health later in the year, but died in September.

At 9.10 a.m. the situation from behind at Battalion Headquarters appeared normal once more, and the reserve companies and the Leinsters withdrew. It must be remembered there was still no real communication with B and D Companies. The ground in rear of their lines was almost impenetrable after the bombardments of the last few days. Besides being churned up by shells, there was the appalling entanglement of shattered trees and undergrowth, and the remains of barbed wire. The communication trenches had practically disappeared, having been filled in with débris, and in places blown out of existence.

At 9.45 a.m., Sergeant Smith, the signalling sergeant, who had been sent forward to try and mend the telephone, returned to say the Germans were in the trenches on the left. Colonel Tulloh immediately ordered up the reserve company to a position in rear of B Company, and arranged for bombing parties to advance to turn the enemy out.

9th May   Major Nisbet was told to send a party down the trench to his left, to turn the enemy on that flank, while a party from A Company, under Captain Vicary, was to move up the left-hand communication trench, and attempt to push back the right flank of the enemy. Both parties worked up to within some twenty yards of the enemy, and hurled the primitive " jam tin " bombs, which were the only pattern then available. These naturally stood very little chance against the German grenades, and the attempt failed with considerable loss.

Hostile machine guns were now in position in the enemy's line, and one concealed somewhere in the open on the right flank continually swept the parapet of D Company ,on the right of the main line, and prevented their assisting with covering fire.

Over on this flank one gallant action was noticed at about this time. A number of men who had been wounded up in the forward trench of B Company were attempting to creep back towards the dressing station. One sergeant, already badly wounded, was seen doubling back towards D Company, when he was suddenly knocked over again. Immediately, without any hesitation, Private Gigg, followed by Private Maidmont, both of D Company, jumped out over the parapet and succeeded in bringing him in. For this both men received the Russian Order of St. George (third class).

Lieutenant Sherlock, the Medical Officer, also distinguished himself away to the left during the earlier stages of the German attack. As has already been mentioned, Lieutenant Aplin had been severely wounded in the stomach, but had got back to the main line. From here it was found impossible to move him, as the trench was too narrow for a stretcher. On seeing this, Lieutenant Sherlock ordered the men near by to open rapid fire, to make the enemy keep their heads down, while he and a couple of stretcher bearers worked back over the top, in full view of the enemy's position. They succeeded in getting back safely, but Lieutenant Aplin died of his wounds on the 15th May.

After the failure of the bombing attacks, a counter-attack was organised by Brigade Headquarters. This was to be covered by the 61st Brigade and 96th Battery R.F.A. The plan was as follows. Two platoons of A Company, under Captain Spear, were to form up in the main line trench on the left, and two platoons of C Company, under Lieutenant Rayner (Essex Regiment, recently arrived, and attached to the Battalion), on the right. Both parties were to get up out of the trenches and advance straight on to the hostile position over the open. The B Company advanced party was to assist by sending out men against the enemy's left. Two platoons were to remain in reserve in the main line, while two companies of the 9th Royal Scots were brought up into the second line. The attack was to commence at 3.30 p.m., the signal to advance being a burst of rapid fire from Captain Spear's party on the left. The gunners were to assist by shelling the enemy in front of Stirling Castle from 3.15 to 4 p.m., and the 2nd Camerons, in trenches to the left of the Gloucesters, were to open rapid fire on the enemy at the same time.

Each of the attacking parties was in position by 3 p.m., and ready to advance on the given signal. This was actually given at 3.45 p.m., and the three parties got out of their trenches. There was some slight hitch on the left, but the whole line was soon up struggling forward through the tangle of trees and wire. They were met with a terrific fire, especially from a machine gun at the apex of the wood, and from two more near Stirling Castle. They were able, however, to get up to within 15 to 20 yards of the enemy, and to establish a firing line there. If supports could have been got up at once, there is little doubt but that the enemy, even then, could have been pushed back, but the condition of the ground made the bringing up of more men a very long proceeding, and before they could arrive the attacking party was practically wiped out. Three small parties under Captain Vicary, Lieutenant Rayner, and Sergeant Barber held on some little time, throwing bombs, but in the end they were forced to retire.

Like the bombing attacks earlier in the day, the counter-attack had failed, **9th May** and with very heavy losses to the Battalion.

Captain Dan Burges and Captain Spear were both wounded early in the attack, and whilst ammunition was being passed up the communication trench, Lieutenant-Colonel Tulloh, exposing himself too much, was hit in three places and killed.

No news had filtered through from the advanced trenches where Major Nisbet's party had originally been and signallers were sent forward to try and find out if there were any survivors. After a while these men returned to say that no one could be found and that the whole line up in front appeared to have been entirely blotted out. Hearing this, Captain Vicary assumed command of the Battalion, and reported to Brigade Headquarters the failure of the attack. General Croker, the Brigadier, realising the impossibility of retaking the trenches with the number of men then available, ordered no further attacks to be made, but that the old main line be cleaned up and improved.

At the time there were left one and a half companies in this main trench, and one company in reserve. Besides Captain Vicary and Lieutenant Grazebrook, there were only three very junior attached subalterns known to be alive and still with the Battalion. Luckily, however, things now became quieter. No doubt the enemy were busy consolidating their gains, and after the struggle and the resulting losses, they could have been in no position to make more of their success.

At about 6.30 p.m. Captain Vicary decided to try and find out definitely about the little force that had been holding out under Major Nisbet. He eventually succeeded in creeping up to the position, and found Major Nisbet, together with Captain Halford, Captain Churchill-Longman, and Lieutenant Steele, with a few men, still alive and safe near the old telephone dug-out. Major Nisbet then crawled back down the remains of the communication trench over the living and dead—a fearful journey, and, as he said, he had " never been so far on all fours in his life." Reporting at Brigade Headquarters, he was ordered to withdraw the survivors from the advanced line, and to hold on in the main trench until relieved later in the evening. The withdrawal was no easy task, especially as in the dark men lost the gap in the wire, and several were hung up for some time. The enemy, also, must have heard the movement, as they sent up hundreds of flares and opened rapid fire all along the front. In the middle of this firing the relief from the 1st Royal Scots arrived, about 1 a.m. on the morning of the 10th. Eventually, however, the line was handed over, and by 3.45 a.m. the Gloucesters, with all their wounded, had marched back to the G.H.Q. Line of reserve trenches, about a mile to the east of Ypres.

The losses of the Gloucestershire Regiment on this 9th May were probably the heaviest in its whole history. Both Battalions suffered very severely—the 1st Battalion down south at Fromelles, in the disastrous attack on the Aubers Ridge, lost 12 officers and 275 men, while the losses of the 61st in the Ypres Salient on this one day amounted to 5 officers and 140 men.

Special mention must be made of the continuous gallantry of Lieutenant Sherlock and his band of stretcher bearers. But for their efforts throughout the day, and during the evacuation, the number of men lost must have been far greater. The signallers also did magnificent work in keeping up communications; if any could be picked out it would be Sergeant Smith, Lance-Corporal Cullimore, and Private Fortune.

The following wires were received during the day, and help to show the trials and losses of the Battalion were not in vain :—

" To Units 81st Brigade. Following from 5th Corps. 1st Army reports infantry attacked and went in at 5.40 a.m. as ordered, and have already crossed German front line trenches. Following received from 2nd Army. Army Commander desires that you will inform troops the initial success of the 1st Army has to a great extent been rendered possible by the hard fighting of 2nd and 5th Corps during the last few days."

10th May   " To Units 81st Brigade. Following from 5th Corps. Chief desires that all ranks may be informed that their gallant defence is greatly contributing to the success of his operations."

In Sir John French's Despatch, which covered the fighting at this period, he wrote : " On the 9th May the Germans again repeated their bombardment. Very heavy shell fire was concentrated on the trenches of the 2nd Gloucestershire Regiment and 2nd Camerons, followed by an infantry attack, which was successfully repulsed. The Germans again bombarded the Salient, and a further attack in the afternoon succeeded in occupying 150 yards of trench. The Gloucesters counter-attacked, but suffered heavily, and the attack failed. The Salient being very exposed to shell fire from both flanks, as well as in front, it was deemed advisable not to attempt to retake the trench at night, and a retrenchment was therefore dug across it."

The position in the G.H.Q. Line to which the Battalion withdrew in the early hours of the 10th May was about a mile to the east of Ypres, and just south of the Menin Road, near to where it was crossed by the Roulers railway—a spot later to be called " Hellfire Corner."

Arriving here at about 3.45 a.m., they were allotted some 300 yards, and were ordered during the day to improve the system, and to put out wire. Work, however, was found to be almost impractible, as whenever men showed themselves on or in front of the parapet, they were in full view of enemy observation posts about Hill 60, and they were greeted by bursts of shrapnel.

Great 12-inch and 17-inch shells roared over the trenches throughout the day, to burst with huge clouds of red brickdust in the middle of Ypres. The city was on fire in many places, and a heavy pall of smoke drifted over the whole.

In the afternoon very heavy firing was heard from the direction of Hooge, and it was learnt later that the 9th Argylls had been practically wiped out in their dug-outs in Zouave Wood, while the Camerons in Sanctuary Wood had been forced back to the second line.

Considerable work was done by the Regiment by night in the trenches, and wire was put out in front, and in spite of storms of shrapnel, this was continued well into the 11th May. On this day a small draft of 35 men under Captain Fane and Lieutenant Baxter joined the Battalion.

At 6.15 p.m. came the joyful news that at last, after several promises, the Brigade was really going back for a proper rest. Guides were sent back to reconnoitre the road, and all preparations were made to move off at 9 p.m.

At 7.45 p.m., however, orders were received from 27th Division for the Battalion to report to 81st Brigade Headquarters in Sanctuary Wood at once. An immediate move was made, and on arrival, at 9.15 p.m., at Headquarters, it was learnt that the Camerons, holding the left of the Brigade frontage, had been forced to evacuate part of the front line, which had been almost obliterated by enemy's shell fire. The enemy had then thrown in large numbers of troops, and had seized the position, and also a slight mound to the south, from which they could enfilade the trenches to the right, then held by the Royal Scots.

In order to clear up the situation, a reconnaissance was made at midnight, when it was discovered that the enemy were bringing up more troops to the high ground. Two wounded Germans were also captured. It was decided that two companies of the Leinsters (82nd Brigade), who were on the spot, should attack at once, while the Gloucesters were ordered to stand by, with a shovel and filled sandbag per man, to dig a new line from the left of the Royal Scots obliquely back to the second line, to which the Camerons had been driven.

Rumours of the attack filtered back, and the Germans were said to be evacuating the position, but at 3.15 a.m., 12th May, it was learnt that the Leinsters' attack had failed. B Company, of the 61st, some 80 strong, under Captain Fane, was ordered up

to the gap to prevent the Germans from breaking through. At about 4.15 this **12th May** company reached the mound, drove the enemy off with the bayonet, and held
the position under very heavy artillery and machine-gun fire, until about 4.45 in the afternoon, when Captain Fane decided to withdraw. About an hour later, however, the enemy were seen to be massing once more behind the rise, and B Company again took the hill with the bayonet and dispersed the Germans. They did not, however, remain up in front this time, owing to the intense artillery fire. C Company, under Lieutenant Baxter, and one machine gun, were sent up to help hold the line and to allow B Company, who had lost about 30 men, and who were very exhausted, to withdraw.

At about 8.30 in the evening, when it was dark, A Company sent two platoons towards the mound on the left, to act as a covering party while a new trench was being dug. The rest of A Company eventually relieved C Company up in front, while D Company provided two platoons in reserve, in case of further troubles.

Early next morning, 13th May, the whole of C Company was withdrawn to the second line, the heavy losses from the enemy's artillery not being considered justifiable. During this latter operation, Lieutenant Rayner, Essex Regiment, attached, was killed by a shell.

During this day the Germans made an attack north of the Menin Road, about Bellewaarde Farm, and took some trenches held by the cavalry, who had just relieved the 28th Division. The Gloucesters were ordered to stand by ready to move off at a mement's notice.

The following wires were received on the 13th :—

"To Units 81st Brigade. The Corps Commander has just visited the Divisional Headquarters, and says he is lost in admiration at the way the Brigade sticks out the pounding it has been taking. The Divisional General hopes to be able to arrange for some relief shortly."

"To Units 81st Brigade. General Joffre has expressed to the Lieutenant-General Commanding his admiration and congratulations at the gallant stand they have made."

By night various parties were detailed for digging and wiring. Everyone was soaked with the rain which now fell, and which made the locality a perfect quagmire.

On the 14th the Battalion was still being held in readiness to give support to the 80th Brigade, but in the evening handed over this duty of "standing by" to the Leinsters, and took over their sector in the front line. This at the time was only a company frontage.

D Company, under Lieutenant Grazebrook, took over from the Leinsters at about 8.30 p.m., but the relief took some considerable time, as the other regiment had no surviving officers with the company concerned. The sector consisted of about 100 yards of the old second line trench, and a portion of the new and uncompleted diagonal trench in front. The whole was in the woods, and bounded by two rides—on the right were the Royal Scots, in the old front line, though by day their left had to be withdrawn owing to its being exposed to German snipers. On the left were the Camerons, in the old second line.

By night work progressed well, and even by day a certain amount could be done in front of the line, as the enemy were invisible over a slight rise. Their snipers were, however, always ready to pick off any favourable target.

Water at this period was the chief enemy. This was struck below the surface, and it meant breastworks had to be thrown up everywhere.

By crawling to the top of the mound to the left front, the enemy could be seen converting the old British front trenches which they had captured on the 11th.

Whilst reconnoitring on the 15th May, two of the regimental snipers discovered a wounded Leinster private, who had been hit in the thigh, and who had lain hidden for the last three days in a dug-out practically in the German lines.

15th May On the 15th cavalry officers came up and went round the line, with a view to taking over on the 18th.

On the 16th General Snow, the Divisional Commander, ordered a demonstration to be made in the area to worry the Bosche. The first act took place at 5 o'clock in the afternoon, when all available artillery opened on Stirling Castle, the Menin Road, and the far side of the mound in front of the Camerons. The enemy's reply, at about 5.30 p.m., was most unpleasant, and D Company suffered a few casualties.

At 6.30 p.m. A Company relieved D Company in the front sector, while at 8.30 p.m. the second act of the demonstration took place. The plan was that the Royal Scots to the left of their battalion frontage should, on a whistle signal, jump out of their trenches and hurl bombs into the opposing enemy line, and blaze away rapid fire, but without actually getting to grips. At 8.30 p.m. the whistle sounded, but before a man could clamber out of the trench the Germans opened a terrific fusilade of bullets, bombs and flares. The act was not continued.

May 17th passed off very quietly—partly, no doubt, on account of the heavy rain. Work on the line continued until the Regiment was relieved at about midnight on the 18th/19th. After considerable delay the sector was taken over by the 19th Hussars, of the 2nd Cavalry Division, and the Battalion marched back, some $12\frac{1}{2}$ miles, to bivouacs south of Poperinghe. The distance, though short in reality, was found to be most trying in the rain and mud after the five weeks' duty in the Salient, and it was not until 7.15 a.m. that the camp at Buseboom was reached. Even then the whole Battalion was not complete. A Company, which had been up in the front line, was not relieved until 3 a.m., and two of their platoons had to be left behind in Sanctuary Wood for some hours as reserves, owing to two platoons of the 5th Durham Light Infantry getting lost.

On the 20th May Sir John French inspected the 81st Brigade, and made the following speech :—

"I came over to say a few words to you, and to tell you how much I, as Commander-in-Chief of this Army, appreciate the splendid work that you have all done during the recent fighting. You have fought the Second Battle of Ypres, which will rank among the most desperate and hardest fights of the War. You may have thought, because you were not attacking the enemy, that you were not helping to shorten the War. On the contrary, by your splendid endurance and bravery, you have done a great deal to shorten it.

"In this, the Second Battle of Ypres, the Germans tried by every means in their power to get possession of that unfortunate town. They concentrated large forces of troops and artillery, and further than that, they had resource to that mean and dastardly practice hitherto unheard of in civilised warfare—namely, the use of asphyxiating gases.

"You have performed the most difficult, arduous and terrific task of withstanding a stupendous bombardment by heavy artillery, probably the fiercest artillery fire ever directed against troops, and warded off the enemy's attacks with magnificent bravery.

"By your steadiness and devotion, both the German plans were frustrated. He was unable to get possession of Ypres—if he had done this, he would probably have succeeded in preventing neutrals from intervening ; and he also was unable to distract us from delivering our attack, in conjunction with the French, in the Arras—Armentieres district.

"Had you failed to repulse his attacks, and made it necessary for more troops to be sent to your assistance, our operations in the south might not have been able to take place, and would not certainly have been as successful as they have been.

"Your Colours have many famous names emblazoned on them, but none will be more famous or more well deserved than that of the Second Battle of Ypres. I want you one and all to understand how thoroughly I realise and appreciate what you have done. I wish to thank you, each officer, non-commissioned officer, and man, for the services you have rendered by doing your duty so magnificently, and I am sure that your country will thank you, too." **20th May**

The next few days were spent in cleaning up and resting near Buseboom, though the Brigade still remained in reserve to the 28th Division, who were again in the line north of the Menin Road.

At 5.30 a.m. on the 25th May the following order was received at Brigade Headquarters :—" 5th Corps states front of 28th Division and right of 4th Division are being attacked—gas being used. Hold your Brigade in readiness to move at $1\frac{1}{2}$ hours' notice. Gloucesters will be ready to move at half hour's notice in compliance with above."

An hour later the Battalion received the following :—" Prepare to move on Vlamertinghe at short notice." In the evening the Gloucesters were moved up, and by 9.30 p.m. were in Vlamertinghe, $1\frac{1}{2}$ miles west of Ypres. Here they continued in reserve with the Camerons until relieved by the 1/Suffolks on the morning of the 28th. The day previous to this, orders had been received for the 27th Division to proceed by march route to Armentieres, and to come under the orders of the 3rd Corps (Lieutenant-General Sir W. Poulteney).

So, after nearly two months in the Ypres Salient, the 2nd Battalion of the Gloucestershire Regiment, about 550 strong, marched south to the more peaceful and comfortable sector east of Armentieres, where the summer months of 1915 were spent.

The total casualties suffered by the Battalion during this Second Battle of Ypres amounted to :—

	Killed.	Wounded.	Sick.	Total.
Officers -	6	5	3	14
Other Ranks	128	368	77	573

and there is no doubt that in this Second Battle, although it was one of almost continual passive defence, the good name of the Gloucestershire Regiment made by the 28th at Ypres in 1914 was more than maintained by the 61st in 1915.

R.M.G.

BATTLE HONOURS AWARDED

YPRES, 1915.
GRAVENSTAFEL.
ST. JULIEN.
FREZENBERG.
BELLEWAARDE.

HONOURS AND AWARDS

DISTINGUISHED SERVICE ORDER—
    Major (T/Lieut.-Colonel) F. C. Nisbet.

MILITARY CROSS—
    Captain A. C. Vicary.
    Lieutenant R. M. Grazebrook.

DISTINGUISHED CONDUCT MEDAL—
    5794 C.S.M. C. Hopkins, D Company.
    9163 Lce.-Corporal A. E. Stevens, C Company.
    8435 Sergt. A. Cullimore, B Company.
    8352 Lce.-Corporal H. Keegan, B Company.

MEDAL OF ST. GEORGE, 3rd Class (Russia)—
    6762 C.Q.M.S. J. Shipway.
    10519 Lce.-Corporal E. Maidmont. D Company.
    9559 Pte. J. Gigg, D Company.

MENTIONED IN DESPATCHES

April 5, 1915—
    Lieutenant-Colonel G. S. Tulloh.
    Captain D. Burges.
    Captain E. G. H. Power.
    Captain A. C. Vicary.
    Lieutenant W. G. Chapman.
    2/Lieut. H. Rummins.

November 30, 1915—
    Major (T/Lieutenant-Colonel) F. C. Nisbet.
    Captain A. C. Vicary.
    Lieutenant (T/Captain) C. E. Gardner.
    Lieutenant R. M. Grazebrook.
    Captain H. B. Sherlock, R.A.M.C.
    7159 Sergeant W. Smith, D Company.
    9258 Lce.-Corporal C. C. Moreman, C Company.
    8557 Pte. H. Rice, B Company.

OFFICER CASUALTIES

		COY.
Lieut.-Col. G. S. Tulloh	Killed - May 9th	H.Q.
Major R. Conner	W. & prisoner - May 9th / Died - Sept. 7th	H.Q.
Major F. C. Nisbet	—	B
Captain D. Burges	Wounded - May 9th	C
Captain D. J. B. McMahon	Wounded - May 5th	D
Captain H. B. Spear	Wounded - May 9th	A
Captain A. C. Vicary	—	H.Q.
Captain W. V. Churchill-Longman	Sick - May 13th	B
Lieut. C. E. Gardner	—	H.Q.
Lieut. C. S. W. Greenland	Killed - May 8th	C
Lieut. L. H. Cox	Wounded - May 8th	H.Q.
Lieut. R. M. Grazebrook	—	D
Lieut. E. D'O. Aplin	Wounded - May 9th / D. of wounds - May 15th	B
Lieut. W. G. Chapman	Sick - April 22nd	A
Lieut. and Q.M. E. H. Dinham	—	H.Q.
2/Lieut. T. H. Cordes	—	A
2/Lieut. F. McC. Rawlins	—	D
2/Lieut. S. Barker	—	D
2/Lieut. B. E. Brenan	Killed - April 18th	C
2/Lieut. F. Steele	—	B
2/Lieut. G. B. Rayner - joined April 15th	Killed - May 12th	C
Captain G. M. Halford - April 30th	—	A
Lieut. J. T. Witts - April 30th	—	C
Captain J. Fane - May 11th	—	B
Lieut. D. Baxter - May 11th	Sick - May 14th	C

CASUALTIES AND DRAFTS

	CASUALTIES.									DRAFTS.	
	OFFICERS.				OTHER RANKS.				TOTAL.		
	K.	W.	P.	S.	K.	W.	P.	S.	O.	O.R's.	O.	O.R's.
Dec. 19	—	—	—	—	—	—	—	—	—	—	25	782
January	—	1	—	—	10	23	—	222	1	255	3	186
February	—	3	—	2	22	68	—	142	5	232	2	153
March	2	—	—	2	14	40	—	82	4	136	5	380
Apr. 1	—	—	—	—	—	—	—	1				
,, 2	—	—	—	—	—	—	—	1				
,, 3	—	—	—	—	—	—	—	2				
,, 4	—	—	—	—	—	—	—	1				
,, 5	—	—	—	—	—	1	—	1				
,, 6	—	—	—	—	—	1	—	1			—	95
,, 8	—	—	—	—	2	—	—	—				
,, 9	—	—	—	—	—	7	—	—				
Carried forward	2	4	—	4	48	140	—	453	10	623	35	1596

	CASUALTIES.								TOTAL.		DRAFTS.	
	OFFICERS.				OTHER RANKS.							
	K.	W.	P.	S.	K.	W.	P.	S.	O.	O.R's.	O.	O.R's.
Brought forward	2	4	–	4	46	140	–	453	10	623	35	1596
,, 10	–	–	–	–	2	4	–	3				
,, 11	–	–	–	–	–	5	–	–			–	53
,, 12	–	–	–	–	–	1	–	1				
,, 13	–	–	–	–	–	–	–	1				
,, 14	–	–	–	–	–	–	–	1				
,, 15	–	–	–	–	–	–	–	2			1	–
,, 16	–	–	–	–	–	–	–	5				
,, 17	–	–	–	–	4	3	–	2				
,, 18	1	–	–	–	–	8	–	5				
,, 19	–	–	–	–	1	9	–	1				
,, 20	–	–	–	–	6	11	–	2				
,, 21	–	–	–	–	1	–	–	2				
,, 22	–	–	–	1	1	3	–	–				
,, 23	–	–	–	–	–	5	–	4				
,, 24	–	–	–	–	–	6	–	3				
,, 25	–	–	–	–	2	4	–	2				
,, 26	–	–	–	–	–	7	–	1				
,, 27	–	–	–	–	1	3	–	–			–	11
,, 28	–	–	–	–	1	4	–	2				
,, 29	–	–	–	–	1	5	–	1				
,, 30	–	–	–	–	1	4	–	1	2	161	2	48
May 1	–	–	–	–	–	5	–	–				
,, 2	–	–	–	–	3	–	–	5				
,, 3	–	–	–	–	–	–	–	1				
,, 4	–	–	–	–	2	14	–	–				
,, 5	–	1	–	–	8	33	–	–				
,, 6	–	–	–	–	3	30	–	1				
,, 7	–	–	–	–	–	5	–	9				
,, 8	1	1	–	–	12	59	–	2				
,, 9	2	2	1	–	47	77	–	–				
,, 10	–	–	–	–	1	9	–	–				
,, 11	–	–	–	–	2	12	–	1			2	50
,, 12	1	–	–	–	21	14	1	2				
,, 13	–	–	–	–	–	1	–	2				
,, 14	–	–	–	1	1	3	–	5				
,, 15	–	–	–	–	–	4	–	–				
,, 16	–	–	–	–	–	4	–	1				
,, 17	–	–	–	–	2	1	–	–				
,, 18	–	–	–	–	2	6	–	2	11	413		
Total at Ypres	5	4	1	3	128	368	1	77	13	574	5 —	257

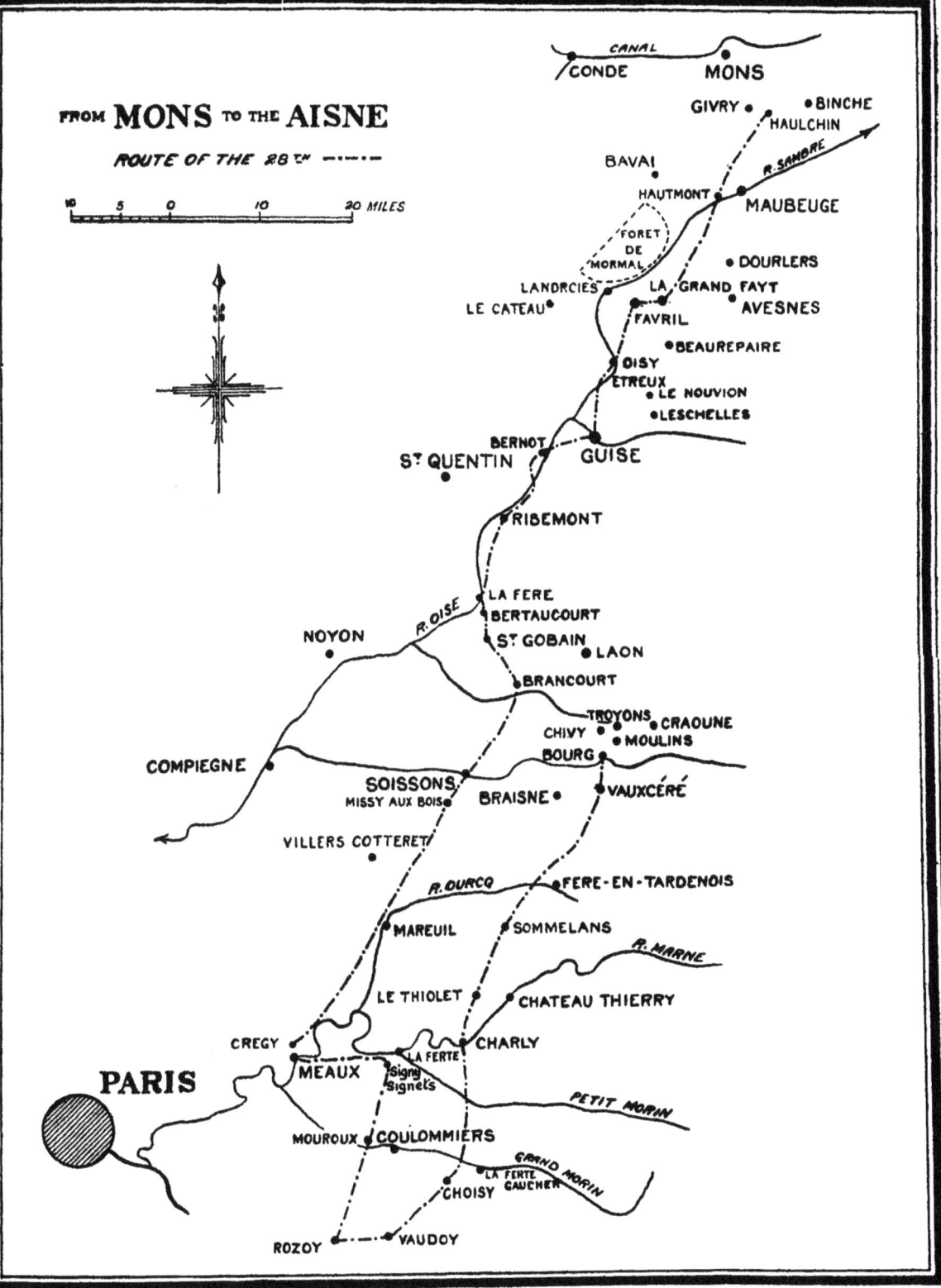

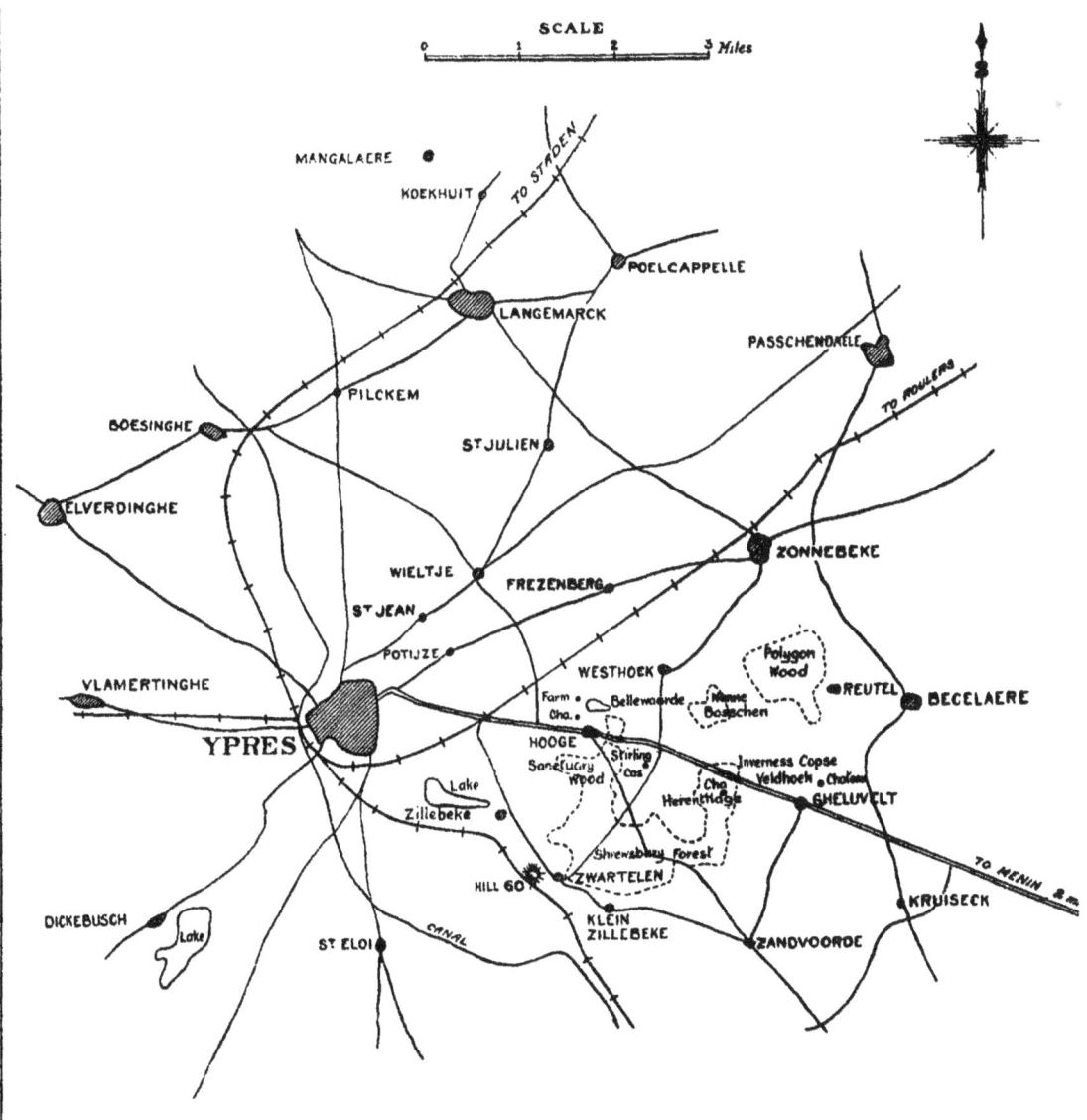

www.ingramcontent.com/pod-product-compliance
Lightning Source LLC
Chambersburg PA
CBHW080601090426
42735CB00016B/3303